Appalachian Cooking

NEW AND
TRADITIONAL RECIPES

Appalachian
Cooking

John Tullock

The Countryman Press
A division of W. W. Norton & Company
Independent Publishers Since 1923

For information about permission to reproduce selections from this book,
write to Permissions, The Countryman Press,
500 Fifth Avenue, New York, NY 10110

For information about special discounts for bulk purchases, please contact
W. W. Norton Special Sales at specialsales@wwnorton.com or 800-233-4830

Manufacturing by RR Donnelley, Shenzhen
Book design by Nick Caruso Design
Illustrations by Alyssa Roberts Comstock
Production manager: Devon Zahn

The Countryman Press
www.countrymanpress.com

A division of W. W. Norton & Company
500 Fifth Avenue, New York, NY 10110
www.wwnorton.com

978-1-68268-100-8 (pbk.)

1 2 3 4 5 6 7 8 9 0

To the brave women who came with their men into the
Appalachian wilderness, who planted the gardens and raised the children,
who cooked and laid by and never wasted, and who made
one-room cabins into loving homes, the author extends his heartfelt gratitude.

Thank you, Mother, thank you Grandma,
and thanks to the many who came before.

CONTENTS

INTRODUCTION

Mention "Appalachian cuisine" to an experienced cook from Flag Pond, Tennessee, or Spruce Pine, North Carolina, and you'll likely receive a blank stare in response. Most of the folks who live in the mountainous regions of eastern Tennessee and western North Carolina continue to prepare dishes that have been enjoyed here for generations. It's just home cooking, they'll say—not "cuisine."

But if you look closely, you'll discover how the influences of southern Appalachia's traditions, long isolation, and climate have molded its foodways, distinguishing them from the recipes of the Carolina Low Country, Creole and Cajun foods of Louisiana, and the soul food of the Mississippi Delta. At the same time, Appalachian cooking reflects hints of all of these cuisines. We cook our greens with ham hocks, but they're more likely to be turnip greens than collards. Black walnuts, rather than the pecans of Georgia, lend flavor and crunch to our desserts. We eat a lot more pinto beans than black-eyed peas. We make corn bread and biscuits to serve with nearly every meal, and we do love barbecue, but we don't do it the same way they do in other places. Cooks from western North Carolina don't make barbecue like their neighbors in the eastern reaches of the state, and East Tennessee barbecue masters have a different approach than their counterparts in Memphis.

In fact, the similarities between the barbecue prepared on either side of the mountains reflects the long, shared history of the mountain people. It's not that other regional cuisines are bad—far from it. We just have our own way of doing things here in the mountains, and we've found no reason to change. Once you become familiar with the flavors of this region, you might just understand why that's true.

WHERE MOUNTAINS ARE KINGS

The Appalachian Mountains were formed in a geologic event that began some 400 million years ago. Running from Maine to Georgia, the mountains reach their loftiest heights in the peaks that lie between North Carolina and Tennessee. The easternmost range, the Blue Ridge, includes the highest peak east of the Mississippi River, Mt. Mitchell at 6,684 feet, and numerous other peaks within the Appalachians that rise above 6,000 feet. Approaching the Blue Ridge from the east you will realize why its abrupt ascent from the Carolina piedmont presented a formidable obstacle to anyone who hoped to traverse it and reach the sprawling American heartland to the west.

The southern Appalachians were never covered by the great ice sheets that crept southward from the Arctic and then retreated about 15,000 years ago. Thus, they served as a refuge for many plants and animals that are now found mostly in northern latitudes. When it comes to spotting varieties of plants and species of animals, traveling from a low valley in the Appalachians to the summit of one of the taller peaks is much like taking a tour up the eastern seaboard to the maritime provinces of Canada.

The mountains have nurtured abundant life throughout their long history. Whole groups of salamanders evolved here, for example, and 100 species of trees are found in the Great Smoky Mountains National Park—about as many as are found in all of Europe, according to information compiled by the National Park Service. When the earliest hunter-gatherers arrived here millennia ago, they found an abundance of game, fish, fowl, nuts, berries, fruits, roots, herbs, mushrooms, and invertebrates without equal elsewhere in the temperate zone. From the first tender, nutritious shoots of pokeweed to the rich, smoky black walnuts in their rock-hard shells to the sweet, spicy, frost-kissed persimmons, the woods provided a bountiful harvest nine months of the year. About 2,000 years ago, the people known as the Woodland Indians began to cultivate crops, including those brought into the region from elsewhere, such as the corn, sunflowers, and squash plants endemic to Mesoamerica, as well as grapes and other native food plants.

The Tennessee Valley region is the cradle of agriculture in the Southeast. Around 1000 CE, the culture of the Mississippian Native Americans flourished throughout eastern North America. The Mississippians built extensive cities, and their often-beautiful artifacts suggest a thriving economy capable of supporting artisans who created objects with more than purely utilitarian design. During the next 500 years, these people perfected the cultivation of corn.

The Mississippians were the first Tennesseans to recognize the value of the area's broad river bottoms for agriculture. They began to construct villages just outside the floodplain, which permitted clearing of large tracts for corn cultivation. They also learned to cultivate the other two crops of the "Three Sisters," squash and beans. Nevertheless, wild foods continued to form a significant part of the Mississippian diet.

The abundance of food led to an increase in population, and gradually, a complex and sophisticated culture emerged. The Mississippian culture was strong in 1500 CE, but with the arrival of Europeans, everything changed.

In the early 1500s, Europeans made isolated forays into the mountains of the South in search of gold. Finding none, they apparently lost interest in the mountains and the people who inhabited them. The earliest recorded European contact with the Mississippian people was in 1540 between the Spanish

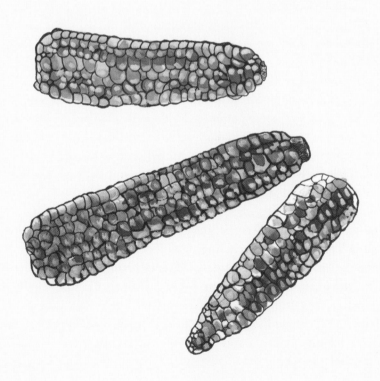

explorer Hernando de Soto and the villagers of Chiaha, about where Dandridge, Tennessee sits today.

Unfortunately, the Spanish brought Old World diseases, including smallpox, that devastated the Mississippians and provoked wars among the various factions that existed within their society. The Cherokee people, who inhabited the Tennessee Valley at the time white settlers began to arrive, were the remnants of a nation driven from its ancestral homeland in the areas now known as Ohio and West Virginia after a long series of wars with the Delaware tribe. The Cherokee had barely established towns along the major rivers of the region when the Europeans began moving in. On the North Carolina side of the mountains, the Catawba tribe continued to dominate, but they too were slowly pushed aside by the relentless onslaught of new arrivals from teeming colonies along the Atlantic coast.

It was not until the 1730s that settlement in the "overmountain" region began in earnest. Colonists began to arrive in western North Carolina and eastern Tennessee from Virginia, and others came north from the Carolina Low Country. The isolation and hardships imposed by the topography there shaped, through both direct and indirect means, the mountain culture and traditions. The mild climate, fertile soils, and plentiful rainfall of the area, combined with its abundance of wild game and fish, influenced the cooking of the region in ways that remain to this day.

Early European settlers in the region included the Dutch, English, and Germans, as well as many (although by no means the majority, as is sometimes claimed) Scotch-Irish people. Between 1710 and 1775, some 200,000 settlers emigrated from Ulster to the American colonies. They were mostly Presbyterians who were seeking freedom from attempts by the British Crown to force them to join the Church of England. The majority arrived in Pennsylvania, and from there they migrated to Virginia and ultimately North Carolina and Tennessee; at the time, the latter was known only as North Carolina's western frontier.

While travel from east to west through the mountains was very difficult, travel through the lower elevations, between the major ranges, was relatively easy. Thus, people from Virginia entered North Carolina via what was known as "the portal," a broad plateau with an elevation of only 2,000 feet that lay between the Blue Ridge Mountains to the east and the Stone, Iron, Unaka, Great Smoky, and Frog mountains to the west. Others passed through gaps in the mountains in the region where Virginia, North Carolina, and Tennessee converge. The early mountain settlers brought with them the values and attitudes that Margaret W. Worley, in her 1913 book, *The Carolina Mountains*, described as "the strictest honesty, an old-fashioned self-respect, and an old-fashioned speech . . . as well as a certain pride, which causes [them] to flare up instantly at any suspicion of being treated with condescension" (quoted in John Preston Arthur's 1914 book *Western North Carolina: A History from 1730 to 1913*).

These characteristics are fully on display among the mountain people of today, along with our dialect, which even in the early twentieth century had changed little from the English spoken in Ulster two centuries prior. My grandfather, for example, would say, "I reckon ye have a p'int," when he meant "I believe you have a point" during a discussion.

Like his father before him, Grandfather was a farmer, in denim overalls and a straw hat, walking patiently behind his team of Percheron horses as they pulled his plow—a man with few capital assets, but with a great wealth of family and spirit. He was fortunate to have received a high school education and to have survived the horrors of World War I as a Doughboy in France; as evidence of his education, Grandfather could easily calculate acreage from lengths measured in feet, rods, or chains—in his head. He taught me to read at the age of four, and to fish at the age of six. He also taught me to be still, to listen to the trills of songbirds, the chitterings of insects, the nickering of the horses in the barn at dusk, the hum of life as it flowed about and through us—a constant reminder that we are part of something much larger than ourselves. This kind of love for the land and its abundance pervades the culture of the southern Appalachians.

Along with their language, the Scotch-Irish brought to the lush mountains their food traditions, inherited from their Old World ancestors. Scottish and Irish foods and cookery can be traced to prehistoric times. The sea provided an abundance of fish, crustaceans, and shellfish. Deer, wild boar, and fowls were plentiful in the forest. Eventually, domesticated livestock arrived, along with the oats, other cereal grains, and cultivated vegetables that traveled westward from Europe, as the people themselves had done.

Fish, shellfish, and dairy products—and, eventually, potatoes—dominated ancient Irish cuisine, and these traditions continued among the settlers after their arrival in the New World. Scottish cuisine emphasized cooked meats, hearty broths, and smoked fish dishes, with nearly all ingredients sourced locally for centuries. In the 1500s, French cooks in the court of Mary, Queen of Scots added rich sauces to the Scottish table. The Age of Exploration later brought wheat, coffee, lemons, spices, tea, and sugar to Scottish and Irish tables.

Margaret Worley, in describing how European customs came to the mountains, reported that "in the late eighteenth century, Georgian hostesses entertained in grand style in their new dining rooms. . . . Wealthy families now offered guests several smaller courses, including soup, fish, game, roast meat, pudding, and dessert." She goes on to say that these customs were practiced by American colonists, as well.

It can be plausibly claimed that southern Appalachian foodways came to America with the Scotch-Irish. Roasted meats and an abundance of vegetables, breads, and sweets continue to dominate the cuisine of the southern Appalachians.

Because of the inaccessibility of the mountains until relatively modern times, the settlers depended on themselves for their food. They had arrived on foot or horseback, and among their meager possessions, they likely brought salt, vegetable seeds, and fruit trees to the Appalachian wilderness. They hunted the abundant game, fished the innumerable streams, and gath-

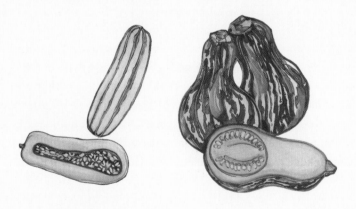

ered nuts and wild greens from the towering forests, just as their ancestors had done from time immemorial. They learned from the Native Americans how to cultivate the "Three Sisters"—corn, beans, and squash—as well as which plants were good to eat, which plants had medicinal qualities, and which plants should be avoided. Native dishes, such as succotash, corn bread, and acorn squash, began to appear on their tables alongside traditional Old World foods.

The late journalist and author John Egerton asserted that Southern food was born when corn, the staple of Native Americans, met the hogs that were brought here by Spanish explorers. This happy marriage is nowhere more obvious than in the foods of the mountainous South. When botanist William Bartram explored the North Carolina mountains in the 1700s, he noted that the mountain people's consumption of corn was exceeded only by that of their livestock. The pig has been revered here for centuries, both in its cured forms—ham, bacon, and sausage—as well as its freshly slaughtered types. The latter achieved its culinary apogee in barbecue, for which cooks on both sides of the Appalachian ranges are justly famous. Barbecue sauce recipes from the eastern and western sides of the mountain are similar, and the Tennessee versions often add whiskey.

As testimony to its prominence in our country's culinary history, eastern Tennessee was once known as the "Land of Hogs and Hominy." In this regard, the mountains also played a featured role; each fall, the lush Appalachian forest produced millions of tons of mast, which enabled farmers to turn their hogs out to fatten up on this free forage. Eons of leaf fall and decomposition produced soils so rich that, when cleared for "newground," they were able to nurture corn crops more luxuriant than could be grown anywhere else.

Similar conditions on both sides of the mountains led to similarities in the cuisine of the mountain people—regardless of whether they paid taxes to Raleigh or Nashville. Where differences in traditional recipes exist, they tend to be subtle.

THE FRENCH BROAD: A COMMON THREAD

For those intrepid enough to undertake the trek, access into the mountains could be gained via one of the two great Native American trails that intersected at a point near the Holston River in what is now Hamblen County, Tennessee. These were known as the Great Warpath and the Catawba Trail. Both can be approximated on modern maps as U.S. Highways 11-W and 25-E.

Their original point of intersection is now covered by the waters of the Tennessee Valley Authority's Cherokee Reservoir, but in the eighteenth century, a fine, large spring dominated the site. There, in 1775, William Bean and Daniel Boone met to scout lands farther west. Ultimately, Boone led a group of settlers northwest, through the Cumberland Gap and into Kentucky. Bean returned to the spring in 1778 along with his family and built a house there. The modest settlement became known first as Bean's Crossroads and later, Bean Station, and it became a waypoint for settlers moving into the western frontier.

Another route across the mountains available to the early settlers was the French Broad River, known to the Cherokee as the "Long Man." The French Broad and its tributaries drain 2,830 square miles in North Carolina and 1,859 square miles in Tennessee, including most of the area covered in this book. The river flows past Asheville, the largest city in western North Carolina, and joins with the Holston to form the Tennessee River just a few miles from eastern Tennessee's largest city, Knoxville. Travel between the two cities followed the course of the river from the earliest days of the republic up until the time when diesel-powered equipment enabled highway construction in places where men with only mules to supplement their strength could not.

Along the course of the river, as well as the other routes that gave access to the Appalachian region, "stations" sprang up to meet the needs of weary travelers. Typically, these businesses operated as taverns serving the locals, as well as inns providing food and overnight accommodations—often three to a bed—for travelers. Along the French Broad in particular, some inns also provided food and accommodations for livestock.

Vance's Station (now a village called Del Rio), located near the North Carolina border, saw as many as 150,000 hogs per year. The hogs were driven on foot from Kentucky and the Tennessee Valley region through the narrow canyon cut by the French Broad and then on to Asheville and the coastal plains of North and South Carolina.

Similarly, hogs were driven along the Great Indian Warpath from East Tennessee to Georgia, Alabama, and Mississippi. The southern plantation states produced little meat, as their primary crop was cotton. Textiles and other manufactured goods were transported back into the mountain regions via the same routes the hogs took. Clearly, the difficulties of these routes were great, as few goods beyond what could be tied to a pack mule made the journey.

The inns with a reputation for good food often enjoyed the most business, but as LaReine Clayton Warden writes in *Stories of Early Inns and Taverns of the East Tennessee Country*: "Long before prosperous innkeepers began to vie with each other in the early nineteenth century for the reputation of a fine public 'table,' private tables had grown bountiful in Tennessee. Before the end of the 1700s, the fertile earth of Tennessee was providing an abundance of vegetables, melons, fruits, and berries."

Consider the menu of an inn in Dandridge, Tennessee, which featured multiple vegetable dishes; an assortment of roasted and cured meats and fowl; several types of corn bread; biscuits; and an array of desserts, from preserves to pies and cakes. This centuries-old tradition of bountiful dining is preserved today in Appalachia's "meat-and-two" restaurants, which offer a selection of proteins along with as many as thirty side dishes. In western North Carolina, inns like the Tapoco Lodge in Robbinsville and the Daniel Boone Inn in Boone are keeping alive the old traditions; their menus showcase the best of Appalachian cooking: Carolina trout and catfish, fried chicken, country ham, biscuits, mashed potatoes, gravy, fried green tomatoes, and other traditional foods are served up on a daily basis. Similar menus can be found at restaurants in towns large and small on both sides of the mountains.

Home tables were scarcely less abundant. In *The Tall Woman*, Wilma Dykeman describes a Fourth of July picnic circa 1880 thusly: "There was a succulent stewed hen and a baked ham, the fresh bread wrapped in a white cloth, corn pudding, pickled beans and vinegar pie, berry cobbler and fruit cakes: plain sweet layers with applesauce between each layer." This was but one family's contribution to the community feast. The whole thing must have been quite a sight. Mountain folks' tables are similar to this day. I remember family reunions at which these same dishes, and many more, were featured. The cake Dykeman mentions is an Apple Stack Cake (page 148) like the ones we make today.

FRONTIER TO DIGITAL AGE

As the Gilded Age was giving way to the twentieth century, the area around Knoxville, Tennessee was sometimes referred to as the "asparagus patch." Among the many farms along the rivers of East Tennessee, those in the vicinity of Knoxville were regarded as having superior-quality produce. Back then, everyone knew that asparagus requires deep, rich soil in order to flourish.

A few miles east of Knoxville, the French Broad and Holston rivers come together to form the Tennessee River, and the vast "Y" formed by that confluence was surrounded by some of the finest cropland east of the Mississippi. Every few years, floods deposited fresh, rich soil along the river bottoms, renewing fertility. Asparagus, and just about every other temperate zone crop, grows well here.

Dam construction by the Tennessee Valley Authority (TVA), which began in the 1930s, destroyed many thousands of acres of cropland. Farms have returned to the remaining river bottoms, however, and during the last three decades, dedicated people have reclaimed lands and restored soils once depleted by tobacco farming. A new generation of farmers is once again planting orchards and raising vegetables. The region is rapidly reclaiming its "asparagus patch" badge of honor, and a new generation of innovative chefs and home cooks are making both traditional and new dishes featuring locally sourced products.

The rolling, and sometimes steep, topography of the region ruled out the plantation farming that traditionally had characterized much of the South. In the mountains, the main cash crop was tobacco, and the average farm was small. In the river valleys especially, the topsoil was deep and rich, and the abundant annual rainfall—coupled with the mild climate—permitted the cultivation of an astonishing variety of crops. Large tracts of forest provided not only abundant game, but also an array of indigenous berries, mushrooms, nuts, herbs, and flavoring agents. Topography and rainfall also conspired to create hundreds of streams and several medium to large rivers. These traditionally supplied abundant trout and smallmouth bass, but local fisheries have declined significantly over the last few decades. In the high mountains, homesteads were mostly tiny, with only a hog and a few chickens to supplement the bounty of the forest and the products of the garden.

The mountains of North Carolina and Tennessee—and the lands westward across the Great Valley of the Tennessee River to the escarpment of the Cumberland Plateau—were regarded as a cultural backwater from colonial times until the turn of the twentieth century. Railroads first arrived in the early 1850s, bringing in manufactured goods and hauling away timber, ore, hemp, and smoked hams. But the region remained isolated from the rest of the country because of the difficulty of travel. Isolation, and the scarcity of manufactured goods, led to strong traditions of self-reliance. In this region, frugality ranks as a virtue among rich and poor alike, and this tendency is reflected in its foodways, which are rooted in utmost simplicity or in recipes that seek to minimize waste.

Modernity eventually arrived in the mountains, and wrought significant changes. By the late nineteenth century, western North Carolina attracted visitors from the east lured by the spectacular scenery, the cool summer nights, and the supposedly curative properties of its waters—especially at several hot springs. Among those who fell in love with the mountains was George Vanderbilt, heir to a great fortune, who constructed his summer home, Biltmore, on a vast tract of mountains and ridges near Asheville. To this day, Biltmore remains the country's largest private home. Its multiple greenhouses once provided out-of-season tomatoes and pineapples for the Vanderbilt table, and today, the estate continues to produce and sell milk, wine, cheese, and other food products of the finest quality.

The Great Depression hit hard in the mountains, as in the rest of the country. Thanks to their relative self-sufficiency, farmers like my mother's family had enough to eat but they sometimes had to go without shoes or other necessities. My dad's family lived in the city, and, lacking the means to grow food, they sometimes went hungry. The New Deal changed much about the mountains: Jobs supplied by the Work Projects Administration and Civilian Conservation Corps put people to work building trails, shelters, and campsites throughout the mountains, and by and large, these remain in use today. The Rural Electrification Program brought electricity to remote communities for the first time, but recovery was slow. Coal, iron, and copper mines that once provided income closed or shifted to automation. Timber companies eventually cut down all the available trees, retreating only from slopes too steep to manage. More jobs were lost. People moved away, seeking a better life. Many communities within the region struggle with poverty even in the twenty-first century.

Modern technology transformed eastern Tennessee. Beginning with the efforts of TVA in the 1930s, modernization of the region moved rapidly. By the time World War II had come and gone, the mountain South was much like the rest of the country. TV dinners and canned soup began to take the place of traditional recipes, and home freezers replaced the pressure canner and the smokehouse as primary food preservation methods. In addition to newly constructed highways, television instantaneously connected once-remote towns with the rest of the world. Today, Chattanooga, which lies at the Tennessee Valley's southern end, near the Georgia line, boasts the fastest municipally owned Internet system in the country.

When officials in Franklin Roosevelt's administration went looking for an obscure location for a secret factory to build the atomic bomb, they chose a site in the Tennessee hills and built the city of Oak Ridge, literally from scratch. Today, Oak Ridge National Laboratory, which lies in the middle of the region, about 200 miles north of Chattanooga, is home to a world-class supercomputing laboratory.

One of the state's three medical schools is located in Johnson City—part of the "Tri-Cities," along with Bristol and Kingsport, that form the metropolitan hub of northernmost East Tennessee. Knoxville, home of the University of Tennessee, enjoys a vibrant music and arts scene, and as the gateway to the Great Smoky Mountains National Park, the city welcomes millions of tourists every season.

Similarly, the western North Carolina cities of Cherokee, Asheville, and Boone continue to lure tourists to the region. Appalachian State University (in Boone), Western North Carolina University (in Cullowhee), and the University of North Carolina at Asheville keep mountain traditions alive through various programs and attract students from all over the world. In Cherokee, the Museum of the Cherokee Indian preserves the culture, language, and traditions of the Cherokee people. Once mostly the domain of hardy European colonists and the Native Americans with whom they continually skirmished, today, western North Carolina and East Tennessee are vibrant melting pots of diversity.

We southern Appalachians have adopted ethnic foods from all over the world but continue to maintain and respect the foodways of our ancestors. We have sushi and sweet tea, hummus and fried green tomatoes, pho and red-eye gravy. Our street festivals celebrate everything from flowers, art, storytelling, biscuits, and beer to Giacomo Rossini, the classical composer and creator of beef tournedos. In addition to its awesome scenic beauty, the region attracts visitors with its veritable food lover's paradise: organic farms, creameries, bakeries, orchards, farmers' markets, and specialty grocers, where you can find locally made products. Even smaller towns within the region have at least one restaurant devoted to local food. And to wash it all down, the products of dozens of breweries, wineries, and distilleries beckon locals and travelers alike.

During the past two decades, production of artisanal food products in the southern Appalachian region has sky-rocketed. Leading the way is Blackberry Farm, a world-class resort located in the foothills near Walland, Tennessee. Its proprietor, Sam Beall, who died in a tragic skiing accident in 2016, was among the first professional chefs to call attention to the deep history and enormous pleasures of "foothills cuisine." The kitchen at Blackberry Farm has served as an incubator for culinary talent that has made a lasting impact on the world of food—not only across the South, but across the country.

While Blackberry Farm was making international headlines, small businesses across the region were continuing to do what many have been doing for a long time: keeping alive culinary traditions passed down from previous generations. Products your grandmother would recognize, such as canned pimentos from Washington County, White Lily flour (originally milled in Knoxville), and sourwood honey from the mountains, are joined by an ever-growing list of purveyors who capitalize on the abundance of high-quality ingredients available here. Regionally produced cheeses, wine, beer, spirits, charcuterie, pickles, and condiments have proliferated in recent years. Asheville now has so many craft breweries that the industry is able to support the production of local hops and local malt derived from mountain-grown barley.

Family farms have been reclaimed, restored, or, in some cases, simply redirected, to answer the current demand for everything from fruits and vegetables to heirloom grains, heirloom hog breeds, and grass-fed beef. And near the tiny village of Chuckey, Tennessee, on a hillside David Crockett may once have roamed in search of game, is the only commercially successful producer of black Perigord truffles in eastern North America. The food of the mountain South has begun to claim its rightful place as a distinctive and aesthetically refined cuisine that retains the nostalgic simplicity of an earlier time.

WHAT YOU WILL FIND IN THIS BOOK

Good food always begins with great ingredients. When you return home from the local farmers' market with fresh, seasonal produce and free-range chicken, you can easily transform them into memorable meals using recipes that have built the reputation of great cooks for more than 200 years.

I literally cannot remember a time when I was not somehow involved in growing or preparing our family's food. My earliest memories of life on our small farm include gathering eggs, planting beans, and watching my relatives slaughter hogs. I observed my grandmother do everything from killing and butchering a chicken to making biscuits and canning pickles. I remember walking barefoot alongside my grandfather as we trekked to the grocery store with a bucket of fresh eggs. He would trade them with the grocer, who attended our church, for items we couldn't produce on the farm, such as coffee and tea. We picked wild blackberries. We harvested sour cherries from two small trees, and sweet ones from a huge specimen planted by my great-grandfather.

We pitched in with relatives and neighbors to harvest wheat and corn and took them by wagon—at first horse-drawn and, later, pulled by a tractor—to have them ground at a mill. When I was a toddler, the mill was still running on water power from Sinking Creek, but by the time I was old enough to tag along, sitting on top of the corn or bags of wheat, it ran on electricity. To this day, I recall the aroma of freshly processed grain wafting on a late-summer breeze.

By the time I was old enough to join the Boy Scouts, I'd been helping my mother and grandmother in the kitchen for several years, so I naturally gravitated to the role of campfire cook. To this day, I prepare some of the dishes I learned to make while camping in the woods—I even included one Scout camp recipe in my first cookbook, *Seed to Supper*. I continued to cook for myself, and sometimes for friends, while I was in college, and by the time I was in graduate school, I felt capable of tackling some of the more complex dishes I'd discovered while traveling or learned from colleagues whose life experiences were vastly different from my own. In this way, I learned to appreciate the foods of regions beyond the American South, including those of Asia and Latin America. I have continued to taste, cook, grow, and learn during the intervening decades. I could not be happier to see Americans "discover" local, seasonal food, as I have been eating this way for most of my life.

My early experiences on the farm also taught me about efficiency. Every part of a pig was put to use, for example. My grandmother also made use of leftovers, often in remarkably creative ways, as did my mother. Likely because of their Depression-era experiences, wasting food was anathema to all the adults in my life. These influences are reflected in the recipes and advice you'll find in these pages.

The food of southern Appalachia includes much more than icons like corn bread and turnip (not collard) greens. For example, tamales have been around Knoxville for so long that they're considered a local food, even though the tamal is an ancient Mayan idea. Two tamales, served in a bowl and topped with chili, become a "full house," one of the few food ideas that can be definitively traced to its origin in early twentieth-century Knoxville. Fried green tomatoes, supposedly a Southern tradition, did not gain wide popularity until the publication of Fannie Flagg's 1987 novel *Fried Green Tomatoes at the Whistlestop Café*, but today they can be found on many menus. They're often made with Grainger County tomatoes grown not far from where our first permanent settler, William Bean, lies in eternal repose.

In the first chapter of this book, I offer recipes for some essential regional pantry staples that provide the unique flavors of mountain cooking. They also hark back to a time when the survival of a family through the winter depended on its skill at and success with preserving what was available during the warmer months. The arrangement of subsequent chapters reflects the relative importance of different ingredients to the mountain home kitchen. Thus, corn in its various forms and its two sisters, beans and squash, come first, followed by other vegetables. Next come meat, fowl, and fish dishes, and, of course, an array of desserts. I've also included a final chapter with a few recipes for good foods that didn't seem to fit anywhere else but nonetheless help define southern Appalachian cooking.

All my recipes, which emphasize variety and freshness, draw on ideas and preparation techniques learned from the people I grew up with and others for whom it has been my pleasure to know over the years. Many dishes that lend themselves to advance preparation are perfect for picnics, community suppers, or tailgating. I'm also a fan of dishes that can be made once and then enjoyed for two or more meals. I've intentionally avoided recipes that require special equipment: You can make almost everything in this book using a conventional range, some pots and pans, and a few utensils. An electric blender, a stand mixer, and a food processor will reduce the labor effort and speed up the cooking process, but they're not necessary for the majority of the recipes. You will need some special equipment for home canning, including a water-bath canner, jar lifter, and canning funnel. These items are widely available. For safety's sake, follow all home canning recipes precisely. While I have included recipes that are suitable for a special occasion, this book is aimed at home cooks, not professional chefs. You won't find much here in the way of precious presentation or over-the-top combinations of ingredients.

What I hope to show in this book is that southern Appalachian cooking, despite its deep historical roots and its strongly regional character, is never set in stone. Our home cooks and professional chefs revere tradition, but they're seldom reluctant to add their own special touches to recipes that have been served for generations. Great home cooking always was, and remains today, a way for neighbors to engage in a little friendly competition.

Everyone around here knows someone—often an older relative—who has a cooking specialty honed by years of church suppers, tailgate picnics, and family reunions. Restaurants serve up new takes on old favorites—perhaps adding kimchi to a pulled-pork sandwich, or soy sauce to a pot of greens. And each variation is delicious. I have yet to meet a wild blackberry cobbler or a country ham that I didn't enjoy. Some are better than others, to be sure, but all are worth tasting.

Therefore, as we like to say around here, "Come on in and sit a spell, and we'll rustle up something good to eat!"

Chapter One

PUTTING BY

From March through November, the forests and fields of the southern Appalachians yield an unrivaled abundance of wild and cultivated foods. Perhaps the prodigality with which food can be enjoyed for much of the year here renders the deprivation of our winters all the more painful. Valley winters are cool, wet, and gloomy much of the time, but in the mountains, winter can produce deadly cold and impassable snowfalls.

Thus, the art of food preservation has been practiced here since about 9,000 years ago, when the people of the Early Archaic culture dried wild grapes and smoked venison jerky. To these ancient techniques, the Europeans added their methods for pickling vegetables and curing meats, and in modern times, our refrigeration, freezing, and canning technologies allow us to enjoy seasonal flavors long after the blooms of summer have faded.

Bread-and-Butter Sweet Pepper Relish

I devised this recipe using some of the same seasonings used for bread-and-butter pickles. The relish will keep in the refrigerator for 6 weeks. You can use this relish like chow-chow, as a condiment for beans. Also try it on grilled chicken or pork chops.

MAKES 1 CUP

1½ cups finely diced red sweet peppers

½ cup finely diced red onion

2 tablespoons apple cider vinegar

2 tablespoons granulated sugar

1 teaspoon whole yellow mustard seeds

¼ teaspoon celery seeds

1. Preheat the oven to 180°F. Wash and rinse a ½-pint canning jar and place it in the hot oven until you are ready to fill it. Wash and rinse the lid and band and place them on a kitchen towel.

2. Combine all of the ingredients in a saucepan. Cover and place over medium heat. Bring to a simmer, uncover, stir, and reduce the heat to maintain a slow simmer. Cook, covered, for about 25 to 30 minutes, or until the volume is reduced by half. Remove from the heat.

3. Ladle the hot relish into the hot jar and set aside to cool to room temperature.

4. Seal the jar with the lid and band and store in the refrigerator for up to 6 weeks. Wait 1 week for the flavors to develop before serving the peppers.

Sweet Lime Cucumber Pickles

These crisp, sweet pickles can be added to potato salad, placed on a sandwich, or used to garnish a plate of barbecue. Before you begin, review the general instructions for water-bath canning found on page 5.

MAKES 4 PINTS

3 pounds medium pickling cucumbers

1 gallon water

1 cup pickling lime

10 to 12 ice cubes

1 quart white vinegar (5% acidity)

4 cups granulated sugar

1½ teaspoons pickling salt

1½ teaspoons Pickling Spice I (page 19)

1. Wash the cucumbers. Trim the ends and slice them crosswise into ⅛- to ¼-inch slices.
2. Stir together the water and lime in a nonreactive container large enough to hold the water and cucumber slices. Add the cucumbers and set aside to soak at room temperature for at least 12 hours or overnight, stirring occasionally.
3. Drain the cucumbers into a colander and rinse them three times under cold tap water. Place the cucumbers in a large mixing bowl, cover with tap water, and add the ice cubes. Set aside at room temperature for 3 hours.
4. Combine the vinegar, sugar, and pickling salt in a large mixing bowl and stir until the sugar and salt have dissolved.
5. Drain the cucumbers into a colander and return them to the bowl in which they were soaking. Pour the vinegar syrup over the cucumbers and set aside at room temperature for 6 hours or overnight.
6. Preheat the oven to 180°F. Add the pickling spice to the bowl containing the cucumbers.
7. Prepare four 1-pint canning jars: Spread the lids and bands on a kitchen towel and place the jars in the hot oven. Set up a water-bath canner (see method on page 5).
8. Drain the cucumbers into a colander with a large saucepan placed underneath to collect the syrup.
9. Place the saucepan over medium-high heat and bring to a boil. Reduce the heat to medium-low and maintain a slow simmer for 35 minutes. While the syrup is cooking, pack the cucumbers into the hot jars.
10. Remove the saucepan from the heat and pour the hot syrup over the slices in each jar until they are fully covered, leaving ½ inch of headspace in each jar. Remove any air bubbles by running a thin blade around the inside wall of each jar, wipe the rims with a damp paper towel, and seal each jar with the lids and bands.
11. Process the jars in the boiling water bath for 10 minutes. Remove from the heat and set the jars aside to cool to room temperature.
12. Store the jars in a cool, dark place for up to 12 months.

WATER-BATH CANNING

Home canning has been around for a long time, and the procedures have been worked out with considerable precision. It is important to carefully follow all instructions for making home-canned products in order to avoid food poisoning, which can be deadly. Water-bath canning is suitable only for certain foods—namely, pickles and other high-acid foods, such as tomatoes, and high-sugar foods, such as jams and jellies. The acids and sugars aid in the foods' preservation.

You will need a water-bath canner with a lid. The canner should include a wire rack that typically holds six or seven jars; look for one with a sturdy rack that will easily accommodate jars of various sizes. Home-canned foods are typically put up in quarter-, half-, and full pint jars, as well as quart jars. For example, you may want to use quarter-pint jars for fruit preserves, while quart jars make more sense for tomato juice.

All sizes of jars use standard, two-part canning lids; pint and quart jars also come in wide-mouth types, which require a larger lid but are easier to fill with chunky products, such as whole tomatoes.

You should also purchase a jar lifter, which is essential for transferring hot jars in and out of the canner. A wide-mouth canning funnel also comes in handy for filling jars.

Before canning, wash the jars in hot, soapy water. Rinse them well in very hot water and keep them in a 180°F oven until you are ready to fill them. Wash the lids and bands as well in hot, soapy water. Rinse them well in very hot water and lay them out to drain on a kitchen towel on the counter.

Fill the water-bath canner with enough water to cover the tops of the jars once they've been added (in case you've misjudged the amount of water needed for the canner, it's wise to keep a saucepan of boiling water on the stove to add as needed after the jars

have been placed). Before you begin filling the jars, start heating the water in the canner over high heat. It can take 30 minutes or more for the water in the canner to come to a boil, depending on your stovetop. If your tap water is mineral rich, consider adding 1 to 2 tablespoons of vinegar to the water to prevent hard-water scale from depositing on the jars.

After the jars are filled according to the instructions in the individual recipes, wipe the rims of the hot jars with a damp paper towel. To each, apply a lid and then a band, and screw the lids closed until just firmly tight—be sure to avoid overtightening the lids.

If the water in the canner is boiling, you're ready to start the process. As each jar is filled, use the jar lifter to transfer it to the canner rack. When all the jars are full, and the rack has been loaded, carefully lower it into the canner. The water in the canner should cover the jars by 1 inch; if it doesn't, add more boiling water. Reduce the heat under the canner to maintain a gentle boil. Cover the canner and start your timer; you'll find processing times in each of the individual recipe instructions.

When the processing time is up, remove the canner from the heat. Carefully remove the lid, opening it away from you to avoid contact with the steam. Allow the canner to cool for a few minutes and then use the jar lifter to transfer each jar onto a folded kitchen towel. Space the jars ½ inch or more apart to facilitate cooling and set them aside to cool overnight. As the jars cool, you will hear "pings" as each of the lids seals properly.

The following day, remove the bands. Test each jar's seal by pressing the center of the lid; if it doesn't move, the jar is sealed. Replace the bands and store any unsealed jars in the refrigerator (be sure to use the contents of unsealed jars within 1 month). As a general rule, home-canned foods should be consumed within 1 year.

Summer Squash Pickles

This recipe, which may be conveniently multiplied, is designed to use up the abundance of squash you are likely to get every season. See the general instructions for water-bath canning on page 5 before you begin this recipe.

MAKES 1 PINT

1 pound summer squash

½ cup plus 2 tablespoons chopped red onion

1 cup water

½ cup plus 2 tablespoons granulated sugar

½ cup white vinegar

½ teaspoon pickling salt

½ teaspoon mustard powder

¼ teaspoon ground turmeric

¼ teaspoon ground allspice

> Note: Use some of the leftover liquid to make refrigerator pickles—bring the liquid to a simmer and pour it over prepared vegetables, such as onions, carrots, celery, cauliflower, peppers, cucumbers, or a combination of several of these. Once the mixture has cooled to room temperature, seal the jar and store in the refrigerator for up to 1 month.

1. Preheat the oven to 180°F. Wash and rinse a 1-pint canning jar and place it in the hot oven until you are ready to fill it. Wash and rinse the lid and band and place them on a kitchen towel

2. Trim the squash. Cut them into quarters, remove and discard the seeds and then cut the squash flesh into ½-inch cubes. Place the squash cubes in a bowl with the onion and set aside.

3. Combine all of the remaining ingredients in a large, heavy-bottomed pot over medium heat and slowly bring to a simmer. Add the squash and onion and bring to a boil.

4. Reduce the heat to maintain a gentle boil and cook, stirring occasionally, for 10 minutes. Remove from the heat.

5. Using a slotted spoon, remove the squash and onion from the pickling liquid and transfer them to the hot jar. Pour the hot pickling liquid over the vegetables until they are fully covered, leaving ¼ inch of headspace. Remove any air bubbles by running a thin blade around the inside wall of the jar, wipe the rim with a damp paper towel, and seal the jar with the lid and band.

6. If using within 6 weeks: Allow to cool to room temperature and store in the refrigerator.

7. If canning and storing: Prepare a water-bath canner as directed on page 5.

8. Process the jar in the boiling water bath for 15 minutes. Remove from the heat and set the jar aside to cool to room temperature.

9. Store the jar in a cool, dark place for up to 12 months.

Green Tomato and Pearl Onion Pickles

Select only perfect produce for the best-quality pickles. Tomatoes can be used whole if they are as small as a golf ball; they should be halved or quartered if larger. Just make sure they have no trace of ripening, or they may become mushy. The recipe is easily multiplied if you have a lot of tomatoes. See the general instructions for water-bath canning on page 5 before you begin this recipe.

MAKES 2 PINTS

1 pound pearl onions

1 cup water

1 cup distilled white vinegar

1 pound small (no larger than 2 inches in diameter), hard, green tomatoes

2 small whole hot red peppers, fresh or dried

2 fresh whole garlic cloves, peeled

2 teaspoons dill seeds or 2 small dill flower heads, fresh or dried

2 bay leaves

1 tablespoon pickling salt

1. Preheat the oven to 180°F. Wash and rinse two 1-pint canning jars and place them in the hot oven until you are ready to fill them. Wash and rinse the lids and bands and place them on a kitchen towel.

2. Bring a large pot of water to a boil. Peel the onions by dropping them into the rapidly boiling water, cooking them for 1 minute, and then removing from the heat. Drain the onions and refresh them by placing them under a cold running tap.

3. Cut off the root end of each onion. Squeeze the stem end of each onion between your thumb and forefinger while holding it over a bowl. The onions should pop right out of their skins. Discard the skins and set the onions aside.

4. Combine the 1 cup water and vinegar in a medium saucepan over medium-high heat and bring to a boil. Remove from the heat, cover, and set aside.

5. Prepare a water-bath canner as directed on page 5.

6. Pack the onions and tomatoes into the jars. Add to each jar 1 pepper, 1 garlic clove, 1 teaspoon dill seeds (or 1 head of dill), and 1 bay leaf. Pour the hot pickling liquid over the vegetables until they are fully covered, leaving ¼ inch of headspace in each jar. Remove any air bubbles by running a thin blade around the inside walls of the jars, wipe the rims with a damp paper towel, and seal the jars with the lids and bands.

7. Process the jars in the boiling water bath for 15 minutes. Remove from the heat and set the jars aside to cool to room temperature.

8. Store the jars in a cool, dark place for up to 12 months; wait about 2 weeks before using to allow the flavors to fully develop.

Pickled Blackberries

We don't often think of blackberries in savory dishes, but these pickles make great garnishes for all sorts of roasted meats. Try skewering one with a cube of cooked deli ham for a cocktail snack.

MAKES 1 PINT

2 cups blackberries, picked over

One ½-inch piece fresh ginger, sliced

1 small bay leaf

4 black peppercorns

3 juniper berries or 1 shot London dry gin

2 allspice berries

1 cup water

1 cup red wine vinegar

3 tablespoons granulated sugar

1½ tablespoons kosher salt

1 small shallot, quartered

1 fresh thyme sprig

1. Fill a clean 1-pint jar with blackberries and place in the refrigerator. Place the clean lid and band on a kitchen towel.

2. Using a mortar and pestle or a heavy skillet, lightly crush the ginger, bay leaf, peppercorns, juniper berries, and allspice berries.

3. Combine the water, vinegar, sugar, and pickling salt in a medium saucepan and stir until the sugar and salt have dissolved. Add the crushed spices (and the gin, if using), shallot, and thyme and place the saucepan over high heat. Bring the mixture to a boil and then reduce the heat to a simmer. Cook for 10 minutes. Remove from the heat and set aside to cool to room temperature.

4. Strain out and discard the solids and transfer the liquid to a separate container. Chill the liquid in the refrigerator for 1 hour.

5. Pour the cooled brine into the jar containing the berries. Seal the jar with the lid and band and store in the refrigerator for up to 3 months.

Pickled Ramps

If Appalachia can claim an iconic food item as its own, it's the ramp. One of the best ways to preserve this plant's unique flavor is to pickle it. You won't need the plant's leaves for this recipe; instead, chop those up and add them to a soup or a stir fry, where they'll impart their unique onion-and-garlic flavor. You can find dried galangal and Szechuan peppercorns at Asian markets or online.

MAKES 1 PINT

1 quarter-size dried galangal piece

1 bay leaf

3 Szechuan peppercorns

2 allspice berries

1 dozen ramps (about 6 ounces)

½ cup water

½ cup rice vinegar

½ cup granulated sugar

4 teaspoons salt

1. Preheat the oven to 180°F. Wash and rinse a 1-pint canning jar and place it in the hot oven until you are ready to fill it (at least 10 minutes, or until it is too hot to touch). Wash and rinse the lid and band and place them on a kitchen towel.

2. Place the galangal, bay leaf, peppercorns, and allspice berries in the hot jar.

3. Trim the leaves off the ramps, leaving only the white parts (see headnote). Place the white parts upright in the jar, leaving ¼ inch of headspace.

4. Combine the water, vinegar, sugar, and salt in a saucepan, stirring until the sugar and salt have dissolved. Cover and place over medium heat. Bring to a simmer and remove from the heat.

5. Pour the hot pickling liquid over the ramps in the jar. Set aside to cool for 5 minutes.

6. Seal the jar with the lid and band and set aside to cool to room temperature.

7. Store in the refrigerator for up to 3 months. Wait 3 weeks for the flavors to develop before using the pickled ramps.

RAMPS

Ramps have a flavor somewhere between onions and garlic, with a piquancy you are unlikely to forget. America's only native onion, ramps are commonly found in cool, rich, and moist mountain forests. They can survive at lower elevations, but never produce the kind of luxuriant stands you'll find in the mountains. Ramps are now cultivated commercially and appear on the shelves of specialty supermarkets in spring.

For generations, mountain folks have trekked into the woods each spring to bring home a mess of ramps. When harvested properly, part of the ramp's onion-like bulb remains in the ground, so it can produce a future crop.

For a taste of wild ramps, consider attending the Flag Pond Ramp Festival, which is held each May in Flag Pond, Tennessee. The annual event features live music, and you'll be able to enjoy a local favorite there: fried, chopped ramps folded together with scrambled eggs and accompanied by fried potatoes, corn bread, and bacon.

Pickled Eggs

In my mother's kitchen, pickling eggs was the standard way to reuse beet pickle brine. The beet juice would tint the whites pink, which made a pretty contrast with the yellow yolk. This recipe has no coloring agent, but you can easily incorporate one (see Note).

MAKES 1 QUART

1 cup plus 3 tablespoons apple cider vinegar

⅔ cup granulated sugar

½ cup water

One 2-inch cinnamon stick

1 teaspoon whole allspice berries

½ teaspoon salt

6 large eggs, hard boiled and peeled (see page 176)

Note: If you'd like to color the egg whites pink, add a cooked, peeled beet to the jar before adding the eggs. If you'd prefer them to be yellow, add 1 teaspoon ground turmeric instead.

1. Preheat the oven to 180°F. Wash and rinse a 1-quart canning jar and place it in the hot oven until you are ready to fill it. Wash and rinse the lid and band and place them on a kitchen towel.

2. Combine all of the ingredients except the eggs in a saucepan over medium heat and bring to a gentle boil, stirring until the sugar and salt have dissolved. Reduce the heat to a simmer and cook for 15 minutes. Remove from the heat and discard the cinnamon stick.

3. Place the eggs in the hot jar. Pour the hot pickling liquid over the eggs until they are fully covered, leaving ½ inch of headspace in the jar. Remove any air bubbles by running a thin blade around the inside walls of the jar and set aside to cool for a few minutes.

4. Seal the jar with the lid and band and set aside to cool to room temperature.

5. Store the jar in the refrigerator for up to 6 months; wait about 1 week before using to allow the flavors to fully develop.

Pickled Hot Dogs

When I was growing up, P. D. Taylor's General Store was about a mile-long walk from my grandparents' farmhouse. Most days, after the midday meal (we called it "dinner," not "lunch") my uncle and I would walk down to the store. My uncle always had a bottle of Dr. Enuf, a soft drink still made to this day in Johnson City, Tennessee, and I would have a Coke. Both beverages cost a dime. For an extra nickel, we could buy a pickled sausage from the jar Mr. Taylor kept on the counter. He would fish one out with a pair of tongs, wrap it in a square of waxed paper, and, if you liked, add a blot of mustard from a squirt bottle he kept handy. This scenario was repeated in countless little roadside stores all across southern Appalachia, and many of us have never outgrown our taste for this salty, sour, umami-laden treat. Choose your hot dogs carefully, as the better they are, the better these pickles will be.

MAKES 1 PINT

⅔ cup apple cider vinegar

2 tablespoons granulated sugar

1 teaspoon canola oil

4 all-beef uncured hot dogs

2 teaspoons Pickling Spice II (page 19)

Note: If you like, you can include bite-size pieces of red onions or sweet or hot peppers in the jar as well.

1. Preheat the oven to 180°F. Wash and rinse a 1-pint canning jar and place it in the hot oven until you are ready to fill it. Wash and rinse the lid and band and place them on a kitchen towel.

2. Combine the vinegar, sugar, and oil in a saucepan over medium heat and bring to a gentle boil, stirring until the sugar has dissolved. Remove from the heat.

3. Cut each hot dog into three pieces and combine the sliced hot dogs and pickling spice in the hot jar. Pour the hot pickling liquid over the hot dogs until they are fully covered, leaving ½ inch of headspace in the jar. Remove any air bubbles by running a thin blade around the inside walls of the jar and set aside to cool to room temperature.

4. Seal the jar with the lid and band and store the jar in the refrigerator for up to 3 weeks.

Celery Vinegar

In the mountains, celery was enjoyed only when it was in season until the early 1960s—but a few gardeners went to the extra trouble necessary to bring in an additional crop in early summer. When it was available, celery could be dried, canned (often along with other ingredients in soup), or made into a syrup or vinegar. Making celery vinegar these days is a good way to use up pale inner stalks with lots of leaves. Use this vinegar on salad, to finish a fillet of fish, or to add a celery note to a quick pickle recipe.

MAKES 1 CUP

1 cup rice vinegar

1 teaspoon celery seeds

¾ teaspoon kosher salt

¾ teaspoon granulated sugar

1 cup finely chopped inner stalks of celery, with leaves

1. Preheat the oven to 180°F. Wash and rinse a 1-pint canning jar and place it in the hot oven until you are ready to fill it. Wash and rinse the lid and band and place them on a kitchen towel.

2. Combine the vinegar, celery seeds, salt, and sugar in a saucepan over medium-high heat and bring to a gentle boil, stirring until the salt and sugar have dissolved. Reduce the heat to medium-low, add the chopped celery, and cook at a simmer for 10 minutes. Remove from the heat.

3. Pour the entire contents of the pan into the hot jar, leaving ½ inch of headspace in the jar. Remove any air bubbles by running a thin blade around the inside walls of the jar and set aside to cool to room temperature.

4. Seal the jar with the lid and band and store the jar in the refrigerator for up to 3 months; wait about 1 week before using to allow the flavors to fully develop.

Homemade Hot Sauce

Small-fruited chile pepper plants typically generate lots and lots of peppers. Use only ripe red ones for this recipe, or the sauce will take on a brownish color. You can make this with only one variety of chile, or you can mix and match.

MAKES 2½ CUPS

1 pound stemmed fresh, ripe small chiles (such as jalapeño, serrano, cayenne, or habanero)

2 tablespoons kosher salt

1½ cups distilled white vinegar

1.　Preheat the oven to 180°F. Wash and rinse a 1-quart canning jar and place it in the hot oven until you are ready to fill it. Wash and rinse the lid and band and place them on a kitchen towel.

2.　Pulse the chiles and salt in a food processor until a coarse puree forms. Alternatively, chop the chiles finely using a kitchen knife, then combine them with the salt. Transfer the puree to the jar, place the lid on top and loosely screw on the band, and set aside at room temperature for 12 hours, allowing the puree to ferment slightly.

3.　Open the jar and stir in the vinegar. Once again, place the lid on top and loosely screw on the band. Set aside at room temperature for at least 1 day and up to 7 days (the sauce will get stronger as it sits, so taste every day and finish when you think it's right).

4.　Return the mixture to a food processor or blender and puree until smooth, about 1 minute. Alternatively, grind the puree with a mortar and pestle.

5.　Strain the mixture through a sieve into a clean glass bottle with a lid.

6.　Seal the bottle and store in the refrigerator for up to 4 months. The sauce will become thinner and may separate after you strain it, so shake vigorously before each use.

Homemade Beer Mustard

Craft beer is on the rise, and it lends a special kick to this spicy mustard. Weigh out the mustard seeds if you can, as it's much more precise. For the beer, I use Saw Works Rocky Hop IPA, which is brewed in Knoxville. Highland Brewing in Asheville also makes a good IPA. I'm partial to IPAs with plenty of hops and a citrus note or two. This recipe requires a blender; it is difficult to make without one.

MAKES 2 CUPS

½ cup plus 2 tablespoons India pale ale (IPA) beer

¼ cup plus 1 tablespoon (1½ ounces) whole brown mustard seeds

¼ cup (1½ ounces) whole yellow mustard seeds

½ cup malt vinegar

1 tablespoon ground yellow mustard

1 tablespoon dark brown sugar

1 tablespoon kosher salt

1 teaspoon onion powder

Freshly ground black pepper

1. Preheat the oven to 180°F. Wash and rinse a 1-pint canning jar and place it in the hot oven until you are ready to fill it (at least 10 minutes, or until it is too hot to touch). Wash and rinse the lid and band and place them on a kitchen towel.

2. Combine the beer and mustard seeds in the jar, seal with the lid and band, and set aside at room temperature for 1 day.

3. Open the jar and add the remaining ingredients. Stir well, reseal with the lid and band, and store in the refrigerator for 1 month.

4. Transfer the mustard to a blender and puree on high speed until the mixture is as grainy or smooth as you prefer.

5. Transfer the mustard to a clean container with a lid, seal, and store in the refrigerator for up to 6 months.

Dry Seasoning Mixes

These mixtures will impart authentic regional flavor to many Appalachian dishes, and all can be multiplied easily. Identify your favorites, make them in quantity, and store them in tightly sealed jars in the pantry for up to 1 year.

Barbecue Dry-Rub Seasoning

Apply this dry rub to ribs or pork shoulder and allow the meat to sit overnight in the refrigerator before cooking. Use about 1 tablespoon of the mixture for a rack of ribs.

MAKES 5 TABLESPOONS

1 tablespoon freshly ground black pepper

1 tablespoon garlic powder

1 tablespoon onion powder

1 tablespoon smoked Spanish paprika

1 tablespoon sweet paprika

1 teaspoon ground red pepper, such as cayenne, or more to taste

Combine all of the ingredients in a small jar with a tight-fitting lid and shake well to combine. Tightly seal the lid and store at room temperature for up to 1 year.

Highland Heat Seasoning

This combination of ground peppers can be used to add heat to any recipe.

MAKES APPROXIMATELY 2 TABLESPOONS

¼ ounce dried whole cayenne pepper pods

¼ ounce dried whole Thai pepper pods

¼ ounce Szechuan peppercorns

1.   Remove the stems and most of the seeds from the cayenne peppers. Remove any stems you find on the Thai peppers.
2.   Combine all of the ingredients and grind in a spice grinder. Transfer to a small jar with a tight-fitting lid and shake well to combine. Tightly seal the lid and store at room temperature for up to 1 year.

Creole Three Seasoning

We have adopted some Creole classics as our own here in the mountain South. Gumbo turns up on menus all the time, for example. This spice combination is the secret to many Cajun and Creole dishes, and it adds zip wherever you choose to use it. Use 3 parts mix to 1 part salt when seasoning soups, stews, and casseroles, or use it without salt as a dry rub for meat, poultry, or shellfish before sautéing or roasting.

MAKES 6 TABLESPOONS

2 tablespoons garlic powder

2 tablespoons onion powder

2 tablespoons ground sweet paprika

Combine all of the ingredients in a small jar with a tight-fitting lid and shake well to combine. Tightly seal the lid and store at room temperature for up to 1 year.

Tamale Seasoning

One batch of this mixture is enough seasoning for 2 pounds of meat for tamales. This seasoning can also be used to season ground beef or turkey for tacos.

MAKES 5 TABLESPOONS

1 teaspoon cumin seeds

2 tablespoons chile powder

1½ teaspoons garlic powder

1½ teaspoons onion powder

1½ teaspoons smoked Spanish paprika

1½ teaspoons sweet paprika

1½ teaspoons kosher salt

1 teaspoon whole black peppercorns, ground

1. Toast the cumin seeds in a small, heavy skillet over medium-high heat until they are fragrant and lightly browned, making sure to constantly stir and toss the seeds to prevent burning. Remove from the heat.

2. Transfer the seeds to a heatproof bowl and set aside to cool to room temperature.

3. Grind the seeds in a spice grinder, return them to the bowl, and add the remaining ingredients. Stir until thoroughly combined.

4. Transfer the contents of the bowl to a small jar with a tight-fitting lid and shake well to combine. Tightly seal the lid and store at room temperature for up to 1 year.

Pickling Spice I

This spice mixture is perfect with sweet or sweet-and-sour dishes, such as cucumber pickles or even boiled corned beef.

MAKES APPROXIMATELY 5 TABLESPOONS

Two 3-inch cinnamon sticks, broken up with a heavy skillet or mallet

4 dried bay leaves, crumbled

1 tablespoon yellow mustard seeds

2 teaspoons black peppercorns

1 teaspoon whole allspice

1 teaspoon whole coriander seeds

1 teaspoon whole cloves

½ teaspoon dried ginger root

¼ teaspoon hot red pepper flakes

Combine all of the ingredients in a small jar with a tight-fitting lid and shake well to combine. Tightly seal the lid and store at room temperature for up to 1 year.

Pickling Spice II

Use this spice mix to make pickles that are more sour than sweet. The savory and herbal flavors will come through. The recipe makes enough seasoning to pickle 4 cups of prepared vegetables.

MAKES 4 TABLESPOONS

1½ teaspoons brown mustard seeds

1½ teaspoons caraway seeds

1½ teaspoons celery seeds

1½ teaspoons coriander seeds

1½ teaspoons fennel seeds

1½ teaspoons kosher salt

2 teaspoons dill seeds

1 teaspoon dehydrated minced garlic

Combine all of the ingredients in a small jar with a tight-fitting lid and shake well to combine. Tightly seal the lid and store at room temperature for up to 1 year.

Barbecue Sauces

Barbecue sauces are similar on the east and west sides of the Appalachians. In western North Carolina, they like a little more vinegar, a reflection of the vinegar-based sauces found farther east on the coastal plain. In eastern Tennessee, we like to sweeten it up a bit—in my version, with a touch of sorghum. And Tennessee whiskey has a tendency to improve anything to which it's added, including the cook. These sauces are intended to be brushed on meat just before it's taken off the heat, creating a glaze, or to be served on the side. Do not baste with them or use them as a marinade, as the sugar they contain will burn and impart bitterness.

BASIC SAUCE MAKES APPROXIMATELY 1¾ CUPS

2 teaspoons cumin seeds

1 cup ketchup

⅓ cup yellow mustard

2 tablespoons apple cider vinegar

2 tablespoons Worcestershire sauce

2 teaspoons hot sauce or to taste

2 teaspoons sweet paprika

2 teaspoons garlic powder

2 teaspoons onion powder

1. Toast the cumin seeds in a small, heavy skillet over medium-high heat until they are fragrant and lightly browned, making sure to constantly stir and toss the seeds to prevent burning. Remove from the heat.

2. Transfer the seeds to a heatproof bowl and set aside to cool to room temperature.

3. Grind the seeds in a spice grinder, return them to the bowl, and add the remaining ingredients. Stir until thoroughly combined.

4. Either proceed with one of the variations on this page or transfer the contents of the bowl to a bottle with a tight-fitting lid and shake well to combine. Tightly seal the lid and store for up to 6 months in the refrigerator; the sauce is best when it has chilled for at least 1 day.

VARIATIONS

Western North Carolina—Style Sauce

To the basic sauce recipe, add 1 tablespoon apple cider vinegar and 1 tablespoon freshly squeezed lemon juice.

East Tennessee—Style Sauce

To the basic sauce recipe, add 1 tablespoon sorghum and 1½ ounces Tennessee whiskey. After combining all of the ingredients, transfer the sauce to a small saucepan over low heat and bring to a simmer, stirring once or twice as it cooks. This last step cooks off most of the alcohol in the whiskey and can be omitted if desired.

Mushroom Catsup

This recipe is adapted from my great-grandmother's copy of *The White House Cookbook*, which was originally published in the late nineteenth century and has been republished in many editions. Use the mushrooms typically sold for stuffing—the larger, the better. Mushroom Catsup adds a special note to my Prosciutto-Wrapped Shrimp (page 144).

MAKES APPROXIMATELY ¼ CUP

10 to 12 ounces large fresh button mushrooms

½ teaspoon salt

⅛ teaspoon freshly ground black pepper

¹⁄₁₆ teaspoon ground allspice

1 whole clove

1. Finely chop the mushrooms or chop them in a food processor. Transfer them to a bowl, add the salt, and refrigerate overnight.
2. Using a strainer and the back of a spoon, press the mushrooms to extract and reserve their liquid; transfer the liquid to a second container. Return the mushrooms to the bowl and refrigerate the mushrooms and the liquid overnight.
3. Repeat this procedure for a total of three pressings over the course of 3 days. The mushrooms should yield ½ cup of juice; if not, add enough water to yield ½ cup. Discard the mushrooms.
4. Transfer the liquid to a saucepan over medium heat. Add the spices and bring to a gentle boil. Reduce the heat to medium-low and simmer until the liquid's volume is reduced by half. Remove from the heat and discard the clove. Set aside to cool to room temperature.
5. Transfer the contents of the bowl to a bottle with a tight-fitting lid and shake well to combine. Tightly seal the lid and store for up to 3 months in the refrigerator.

Heirloom Tomato Chutney

A condiment for all seasons, chutney goes great with roasted meats. This one might also accompany a spicy vegetarian curry.

MAKES APPROXIMATELY 2 CUPS

2 pounds firm, ripe heirloom tomatoes, peeled, cored, and cut into chunks

½ teaspoon kosher salt

1 Jonagold apple, cored and chopped into 1-inch chunks

½ teaspoon freshly squeezed lemon juice

2 teaspoons sunflower oil

1 medium onion, sliced into half moons

½ cup diced green tomato

2 tablespoons light brown sugar

1 teaspoon fresh lemon zest, removed in long shreds with a bar zester

½ teaspoon ground cinnamon

1 cup diced bell pepper, any color

1. Place the ripe tomatoes in a large colander set over a bowl and toss with the salt. Set aside to collect the liquid while you complete the recipe.

2. Combine the apple and lemon juice in a bowl and toss well to prevent darkening. Set aside.

3. Warm the oil in a heavy, 4-quart pot over medium heat. Add the onion and cook, stirring occasionally, until golden. Add the apple and green tomato and sauté for 3 minutes. Add the brown sugar, lemon zest, and cinnamon and stir well. Add the bell peppers and reserved ripe tomatoes and stir until well combined. (Save the tomato juice to add to a soup.)

4. Reduce the heat to low and cook at a slow simmer, stirring now and then, until the chutney has thickened to a jam-like consistency. Remove from the heat and set aside to cool to room temperature.

5. Transfer the contents of the pot to a clean 1-pint canning jar. Tightly seal the lid and store for up to 3 months in the refrigerator.

Oven-Dried Apples

My grandmother dried the tart June apples that grew in her orchard using what we called a "tobacco canvas," a cheesecloth-like material, stretched across a pair of sawhorses. Our neighbors used a screen door for the same purpose. These days, you can purchase a fancy dehydrator to do the job, or you can just use your oven. Commercially dried apples tend to be made from only a few varieties—notably, Granny Smith. For this recipe, I encourage you to seek out classic cooking apple varieties, such as McIntosh, Empire, and Cortland, or, better yet, use locally grown heirloom apples. The drying process caramelizes some of the sugar in the apples and concentrates their flavor, and the result is like no other preserved apple. I used Cortland apples when developing this recipe, and five medium apples filled two baking sheets with rings and left a nice piece for me to snack on. You'll need to adjust your baking time depending on the variety of apple you choose; Cortland apples have firm, crisp, and pure white flesh that doesn't brown easily, and juicier apples may require a longer drying time.

MAKES APPROXIMATELY 1 PINT

5 medium apples

1. Preheat the oven to 200°F and line 2 baking sheets with wax paper.
2. Peel, core, and slice the apples into ⅛-inch rings. Place the rings on the prepared baking sheets, place the sheets on separate shelves in the oven, and bake for 1 hour.
3. Swap the positions of the baking sheets in the oven and bake for 1 hour more. Remove from the oven and set aside at room temperature overnight.
4. Check to see if the apples are leathery, neither flabby nor crisp. Remove any that have reached this point and return any others to a 200°F oven and bake for 45 minutes to 1 hour, or until pale golden brown and leathery. Remove from the oven and cool completely.
5. Store in a sealed, airtight container. The apples will keep for 1 month at room temperature, or can be frozen for much longer.

GREASY BEANS

Numerous heirloom vegetables have been preserved by Appalachian gardeners, and in recent years, several companies specializing in heirloom seeds have made them available to modern growers (see Sources, page 183). Among the many varieties of beans seed savers have collected are so-called "greasy" beans, which are meaty and flavorful and keep well after picking—much better than standard green beans. This bean variety lacks the tiny hairs on the pods, which gives them a shiny, slick appearance and a greasy feel. Their ability to resist mold has no doubt contributed to their popularity in making leather britches. Greasy beans have been cultivated on both sides of the mountains for generations.

Leather Britches

Leather britches, or shuck beans, were much more common in the days before home canning became possible. No one knows for sure how they came to be called "leather britches," but the tough, leathery texture of the finished product surely must have played a role. The technique for drying whole green beans to preserve them was apparently introduced by German settlers in the eighteenth century. Late-season beans, with seeds beginning to swell the pods, make the finest-tasting leather britches. Among the best varieties of beans for this recipe are October beans, cornfield beans, white half runners, and greasy beans, but big, hefty, Italian-type green beans should also work. A food dehydrator speeds up the process, but you can easily make leather britches the old-fashioned way without one (see Note). Leather britches must be rehydrated and cooked to become palatable. For cooking instructions, see the recipe for Shuck Beans with Bacon on page 52.

SERVINGS VARY

Freshly picked green beans

Note: Green beans can also be dried in a food dehydrator. Follow the manufacturer's instructions or simply dry the beans until they are leathery and wrinkled.

1. Using a darning needle and heavy cotton thread, string the beans together by piercing each one near the stem end, as if arranging a strand of beads (strands about three feet long are the easiest to work with).
2. When all the beans have been strung, hang up the strands in a warm, airy place away from direct sunlight. As they dry, the beans will become leathery and wrinkled. They will dry sufficiently in about 3 weeks—after which time you can either leave them hanging or remove them from the strings and store them in brown paper bags at room temperature.

Seeded Honey

Honey is often abundant in fall, when nuts and seeds are also in season. This infinitely variable condiment has multiple uses. Spread it on a biscuit at breakfast, or use it as a topping for cheese. It is especially good with creamy goat and tangy blue cheeses. I hope these variations inspire you to create your own combinations; I'm partial to the honey from Strange Honey Farm, located in Del Rio, Tennessee (see Sources, page 183).

Turkish Delight

MAKES ½ CUP

¼ cup orange blossom honey

¼ cup chopped pistachios

2 tablespoons sesame seeds, lightly toasted (see Note)

All American

MAKES ½ CUP

¼ cup dark wildflower honey

2 tablespoons chopped native pecans

2 tablespoons pepitas (pumpkin seeds), toasted (see Note)

2 tablespoons sunflower seeds, toasted (see Note)

Old World

MAKES ¼ CUP

¼ cup clover honey

1 teaspoon fennel seeds

1 teaspoon sesame seeds

1 teaspoon coriander seeds, lightly crushed

For each variation, combine all of the ingredients in a jar with a tight-fitting lid and shake well to combine. Tightly seal the lid and store for up to 6 months at room temperature; wait at least 1 week before using to allow the flavors to combine.

Note: To toast the seeds, place them in a dry skillet over medium-high heat. Toss and stir until 1 or 2 of the seeds pop, and most are lightly browned. Remove from the heat and transfer to a heatproof bowl to cool.

Onion Jam

I devised this recipe to use up leftover onion trimmings from the Warm Bean Salad in Roasted Sweet Onions recipe on page 56. If you want to start from scratch, use only five onions and follow the directions for roasting them found in that recipe.

MAKES APPROXIMATELY 2 CUPS

3 tablespoons bacon drippings

Trimmings from 6 large roasted sweet onions (page 56), chopped

6 fresh thyme sprigs

3 fresh rosemary sprigs

3 bay leaves

2¼ cups granulated sugar

1½ cups apple cider vinegar

½ teaspoon salt

Freshly ground black pepper

1. Warm the bacon drippings in a large pot over medium heat. Add the onions and cook, stirring occasionally, for 15 minutes, or until all the pieces have browned areas.

2. Tie the thyme and rosemary sprigs and the bay leaves together with cotton string to make a *bouquet garni*. Add the *bouquet garni* to the pot, reduce the heat to low, and cook, stirring occasionally, for 5 minutes.

3. Sprinkle the sugar over the onions and cook, without stirring, for 5 minutes, or until the sugar melts. Raise the heat to medium-high and cook for 4 minutes, or until the sugar is caramelized. Stir in the vinegar and reduce the heat to medium-low. Simmer, stirring occasionally, for 20 minutes, or until the mixture thickens. Remove from the heat and discard the *bouquet garni*. Add the salt and several grinds of the black pepper and stir to combine.

4. Use the jam immediately or set aside to cool to room temperature before storing. If storing, transfer the jam to a clean jar with a tight-fitting lid. Tightly seal the lid and store for up to 3 weeks in the refrigerator.

Red Pepper Jelly

Everyone calls this recipe Red Pepper Jelly, but technically, unless you use only the juice of the peppers to produce a clear finished product, you have a jam, not a jelly. Jams have small pieces of fruit or vegetable suspended in the gelled liquid. The recipe as written yields a mildly spicy jam. You can use a higher proportion of jalapeños to create a hotter product. Just reduce the amount of green peppers accordingly. This jam is an ingredient in Fried Green Tomatoes Sauce (page 75). You can also serve it over goat cheese with crackers for an easy appetizer.

MAKES SIX ½-PINT JARS

2½ cups finely chopped red bell peppers

1¼ cups finely chopped green bell peppers

¼ cup finely chopped jalapeño peppers

1 cup apple cider vinegar

One 1¾-ounce package powdered pectin

5 cups white sugar

1. Preheat the oven to 180°F. Wash and rinse six ½-pint canning jars and place them in the hot oven until you are ready to fill them. Wash and rinse the lids and bands and place them on a kitchen towel.

2. Set up a water-bath canner (see method on page 5).

3. Place the red bell peppers, green bell peppers, and jalapeño peppers in a large saucepan. Mix in the vinegar and fruit pectin. Set the pan over high heat. Stirring constantly, bring the mixture to a full rolling boil. Quickly stir in the sugar. Return the mixture to a boil, and boil exactly 1 minute, stirring constantly. Remove from the heat and skim off any foam.

4. Quickly ladle the jam into the hot jars, leaving ¼ inch of headspace in each jar. Wipe the rims of the hot jars with a damp paper towel and seal each jar with the lids and bands.

5. Process the jars in the boiling water bath for 5 minutes. Remove from the heat and set the jars aside to cool overnight. Store in the pantry for up to 12 months.

Pineapple Upside-Down Cake Jam

Because they were exotic and expensive to grow in the temperate zone, pineapples symbolized wealth in eighteenth-century Europe, and they retained this status among European colonists in America. Many fine antebellum Southern homes have pineapple motifs incorporated into the woodwork—in the entry hall, for example, or perhaps above the dining room fireplace, or on the pediments above the front windows. Canned pineapple produced in Hawaii made its debut on the American table just prior to World War I, and by the middle of the twentieth century, pineapple could be had anywhere. Anyone could enjoy this once-exotic treat, and pineapple upside-down cake has become a favorite way to serve it.

This jam recipe delivers all the flavors of pineapple upside-down cake—in a jar! Make this for Christmas gifts, and your recipients will thank you every time they have a bite. See the general information for water-bath canning on page 5 before you get started.

MAKES FOUR ½-PINT JARS

2 ¼ cups granulated sugar

1¾ cups light brown sugar, loosely packed

3¼ cups chopped fresh pineapple (from 1 whole pineapple, trimmed)

¾ cup pecans

One 1¾-ounce package powdred pectin

½ teaspoon unsalted butter

1 teaspoon vanilla extract

1.   Preheat the oven to 180°F. Wash and rinse four ½-pint canning jars and place them in the hot oven until you are ready to fill them. Wash and rinse the lids and bands and place them on a kitchen towel.

2.   Set up a water-bath canner (see method on page 5).

3.   Combine the sugars in a bowl.

4.   Combine the pineapple, pecans, pectin, and butter in a large pot over medium-high heat, and while stirring constantly, bring the fruit mixture to a rolling boil.

5.   Add the sugars all at once and, while stirring constantly, return to a rolling boil and boil for exactly 1 minute. Remove from the heat and skim off and discard any foam that has formed.

6.   Stir in the vanilla extract and then ladle the jam into the hot jars.

7.   Wipe the rims of the hot jars with a damp paper towel and seal each jar with the lids and bands.

8.   Process the jars in the boiling water bath for 10 minutes. Remove from the heat and set the jars aside to cool to room temperature.

9.   Store the jars in a cool, dark place for up to 12 months.

Berry Preserves

Appalachian cooks did not always have the luxury of a sheaf of recipes to consult whenever a season provided unexpected abundance. Rules of thumb were easier to remember. This recipe for fruit preserves can be adapted to work with any berry you have on hand, from the earliest strawberries to the last of the raspberries, or even for supermarket berries. After preparing the fruit for eating, taste one berry and judge for yourself whether to use more or less sugar in the recipe.

YIELD VARIES

Berries

Sugar

Spices (optional; see Note)

1.   For each cup of fruit, allow ½ to 1 cup of sugar, depending upon how tart the berries are and how sweet you wish the preserves to be. Combine the fruit and sugar in a saucepan and stir them together with a wooden spoon, crushing a few berries to release their juices. Cover the saucepan and place in the refrigerator overnight.

2.   Remove the saucepan from the refrigerator; the berries should be swimming in syrup created by the interaction between their juices and the sugar. Place the saucepan over medium-low heat and slowly bring to a simmer. Allow the mixture to cook gently for 1 minute and then remove from the heat. Set aside to cool to room temperature.

3.   Use the preserves immediately or store them. If storing for a short period, transfer the preserves to a jar with a tight-fitting lid. Tightly seal the lid and store for up to 1 month in the refrigerator.

4.   For longer-term storage, preheat the oven to 180°F. Wash and rinse as many ½-pint canning jars as you will need and place them in the hot oven until you are ready to fill them. Wash and rinse the lids and bands and place them on a kitchen towel.

Note: You may add spices, such as cinnamon, nutmeg, clove, allspice, etc. to the fruit and sugar mixture. Use whole spices tied in a small pouch of cheesecloth as a *bouquet garni* (page 27), so they can be easily removed when the preserves are ready for storage. Be conservative with the amount of spice used; only a hint is needed, as you don't want to overwhelm the flavor of the fruit.

5. Set up a water-bath canner (see method on page 5).

6. Ladle the preserves into the hot jars, leaving ¼ inch of headspace in each jar. Wipe the rims of the hot jars with a damp paper towel and seal each jar with the lids and bands.

7. Process the jars in the boiling water bath for 15 minutes. Remove from the heat and set the jars aside to cool to room temperature.

8. Store the jars in a cool, dark place for up to 12 months.

Chapter Two

THE THREE SISTERS

Corn has been cultivated in Tennessee for at least 1,800 years, and it's probably been grown there since as early as the first century CE. It became the staple crop of the Mississippian Native American culture that dominated the area until around 1500 CE and was subsequently the staple of the Cherokee, who continued to reside in the East Tennessee region until their forced removal in 1838. The Mississippians learned how to cultivate beans and squash along with their corn, and these crops—the Three Sisters—provided the nutrition that allowed their culture to flourish.

When the Europeans arrived in the mountains, they already knew how to grow the Three Sisters, thanks to the Algonquin tribes of the mid-Atlantic region. Doubtless, they were pleased to discover that these crops grew even more vigorously in the rich soils of the mountain coves and river bottoms.

To this day, Hickory King corn, Turkey Craw beans, and Candy Roaster squash continue to feed many Appalachian households; these heirloom varieties have been handed down since colonial times.

Farmers and gardeners in Tennessee and North Carolina plant these and many other varieties of the Three Sisters each season. Read on to learn what we do with them in the kitchen.

Easy Corn Bread

I first learned how to make corn bread using a corn bread mix made in Knoxville. That product is no longer available, but several good brands remain on the market. Most contain cornmeal, flour, baking powder, and salt—avoid any with added sugar. Yellow or white cornmeal is a matter of personal preference. You really need a cast-iron skillet to make good corn bread. If you don't own one, use a heavy, metal baking pan that can stand up to preheating, which is essential to get a dark, crispy crust. You may need to adjust the baking time if you're not using cast iron. Variations on this basic recipe follow.

MAKES ONE 9-INCH ROUND

1 tablespoon bacon drippings or vegetable oil

1 cup self-rising corn bread mix

1¼ cups whole milk, plus more as needed

1 large egg

1 tablespoon vegetable oil

1. Preheat the oven to 425°F.
2. Place the bacon drippings in a 9-inch cast-iron skillet and warm it in the hot oven for at least 10 minutes.
3. Place the corn bread mix in a large mixing bowl, and in a separate bowl, thoroughly whisk together the milk, egg, and vegetable oil. Make a well in the corn bread mix, pour in the milk mixture, and whisk until combined. (If the batter is not pourable, whisk in a little more milk.)
4. Carefully remove the hot skillet from the oven, set it on the stove top, and pour in the batter (it should sizzle). Carefully return the skillet to the oven and bake for 35 minutes, or until the corn bread is golden brown on top and pulling away from the skillet at the edges. Remove from the oven and serve.

Heirloom Corn Bread

Corn has always been an important crop on both sides of the mountains. The Old World grains, such as wheat, oats, barley, and rye, lend themselves to large-scale cultivation with a well-organized labor force, but one man can bring in a crop of corn that's sufficient to feed him, his family, and their livestock. In recent years, several heirloom varieties of corn have reappeared on the market, and any of them can make corn bread with a sweet, nutty taste you could never achieve in bread made with mass-produced cornmeal. Because most heirloom cornmeal is "stone ground," it produces a bread with a coarser crumb. Hickory King corn is a popular variety for cornmeal throughout the mountains, and Tennessee Red Cob corn is a Tennessee Valley heirloom. Either makes exceptional corn bread (see Sources, page 183).

MAKES ONE 9-INCH ROUND

1 tablespoon bacon drippings or vegetable oil

1 cup stone-ground heirloom cornmeal

½ teaspoon baking soda

½ teaspoon sea salt

1 cup buttermilk

1 large egg

1 tablespoon corn oil

1. Preheat the oven to 425°F.
2. Place the bacon drippings in a well-seasoned 9-inch cast-iron skillet and warm it in the hot oven for at least 10 minutes.
3. Whisk together the cornmeal, baking soda, and salt in a large mixing bowl, and in a separate bowl, thoroughly whisk together the buttermilk, egg, and oil. Make a well in the dry ingredient mixture, pour in the buttermilk mixture, and whisk until a uniform batter forms.
4. Carefully remove the hot skillet from the oven, set it on the stove top, and pour in the batter (it should sizzle). Carefully return the skillet to the oven and bake for 25 to 35 minutes, or until the corn bread is golden brown on top. Remove from the oven and serve.

MILLING CORNMEAL

In the southern mountains, one of the earliest signs of civilization was the construction of a grist mill. Mills were essential for grinding corn into meal for corn bread, and the considerable effort required to erect a mill and install heavy millstones couldn't be justified unless a more or less stable group of permanent settlers was nearby. The names of hamlets and roads throughout southern Appalachia often reference their nearby mill.

Cornmeal produced by a water-powered mill differs from modern cornmeal in significant ways; for example, the slow, deliberate motion of a waterwheel and slightly yielding surfaces of millstones keep the temperature of the corn low, which preserves essential oils and flavor. By contrast, modern commercial mills use electric motors to turn steel rollers at high speeds, producing a fine, uniform texture and generating enough heat to alter the flavor. Today, the USDA defines "stone-ground, whole-grain cornmeal" as "cornmeal that contains the bran, endosperm, and germ in the same relative proportions as they exist in the intact corn kernels"—note that it doesn't reference the actual grinding of the corn at all, only the degree to which it remains intact. Meal that is labeled "stone ground" is the best choice for recalling the genuine flavor and texture of traditional Appalachian cornmeal. Store stone-ground meal in the freezer and use it within 6 months.

Blue Cornmeal Griddle Cakes

Griddle cakes were at one time known as "hoe cakes" because they were cooked on the flattened-out blade of a hoe, rather than a skillet, over an open fire. They are also called "Johnny cakes." The blue heirloom cornmeal for this recipe is available from Anson Mills (see Sources, page 183). It is sweet all on its own, without added sugar.

MAKES APPROXIMATELY 10 GRIDDLE CAKES

½ cup stone-ground blue heirloom cornmeal

¼ teaspoon baking soda

⅛ teaspoon salt

¾ cup buttermilk

1 large egg, well beaten

1 tablespoon plus 2 teaspoons peanut oil, plus more as needed

1.   Warm a heavy, cast-iron skillet over medium heat and preheat the oven to 200°F.

2.   Whisk together the cornmeal, baking soda, and salt in a large mixing bowl, and in a separate bowl, thoroughly whisk together the buttermilk, the egg, and 2 teaspoons of the oil. Make a well in the dry ingredient mixture, pour in the buttermilk mixture, and stir until just combined.

3.   Once the skillet begins to smoke, add the remaining 1 tablespoon of oil. Once the oil begins to smoke, ladle the batter into the skillet, making 3-inch diameter cakes (about ¼ cup for each cake). Don't crowd the skillet. When the cakes are bubbly and dull looking on top, flip them to brown the other side. Once done, transfer the cakes to a platter kept in the warm oven.

4.   Continue until you have used all the batter; add a little more oil to the skillet as needed. Remove from the heat and the oven and serve.

Cracklin Corn Bread

"Cracklins" are bits of pork that remain after the lard has been rendered out, and they can add a rich, porky flavor to corn bread. Pair this corn bread with Soup Beans (page 50) for a traditional combination, or try it with Pimento Cheese Chowder (page 171). Cracklins are just one of several additions that can spruce up corn bread.

MAKES ONE 9-INCH ROUND

2 tablespoons bacon drippings

1 cup stone-ground cornmeal

½ teaspoon baking powder

½ teaspoon baking soda

¼ teaspoon salt

1½ cups buttermilk

1 large egg, well beaten

1 tablespoon peanut oil

⅓ cup pork cracklins or crumbled crispy bacon

1. Preheat the oven to 450°F.
2. Place the bacon drippings in a well-seasoned 9-inch cast-iron skillet and warm it in the hot oven for at least 10 minutes.
3. Whisk together the cornmeal, baking powder, baking soda, and salt in a large mixing bowl, and in a separate bowl, thoroughly whisk together the buttermilk, egg, and oil. Make a well in the dry ingredient mixture, pour in the buttermilk mixture, and stir until just combined. Add the cracklins and stir until they are evenly distributed.
4. Carefully remove the hot skillet from the oven, set it on the stove top, and pour in the batter (it should sizzle). Carefully return the skillet to the oven and bake for 25 to 35 minutes, or until the corn bread is golden brown on top. Remove from the oven and set aside to cool for 10 minutes.
5. Serve warm.

Stone-Ground Corn Bread with Corn Kernels

Wapsi Valley corn is said to have originated with the Cherokee. Fortunately, it and other heirloom corn varieties still exist today, as do a few small mills that continue to produce cornmeal the old-fashioned way. Stone-ground meals preserve more of the flavor and nutrition of the whole grain, and also produce a coarsely textured corn bread that many people love.

MAKES ONE 9-INCH ROUND

1 tablespoon bacon drippings or vegetable oil

1 cup stone-ground cornmeal

1 teaspoon baking soda

½ teaspoon salt

1 cup buttermilk, at room temperature

1 large egg, at room temperature

1 tablespoon corn oil

½ cup corn kernels, fresh or frozen and thawed

Room-temperature water, as needed

1. Preheat the oven to 425°F.
2. Place the bacon drippings in a well-seasoned 9-inch cast-iron skillet and warm it in the hot oven for at least 10 minutes.
3. Whisk together the cornmeal, baking soda, and salt in a large mixing bowl, and in a separate bowl, thoroughly whisk together the buttermilk, egg, and oil. Make a well in the dry ingredient mixture, pour in the buttermilk mixture, and stir until just combined. Add the corn kernels and stir gently until they are evenly distributed. If necessary to make the batter pourable, add a little water.
4. Carefully remove the hot skillet from the oven, set it on the stove top, and pour in the batter (it should sizzle). Carefully return the skillet to the oven and bake for 25 to 35 minutes, or until the corn bread is golden brown on top. Remove from the oven and set aside to cool for a few minutes.
5. Serve warm.

Sweet Onion Skillet Corn Bread

There was a time when truly sweet onions were difficult to grow in the Appalachian south, but plant breeders have answered the need, and farmers' markets now often feature sweet onions in late summer. You can make the dish with Vidalia, Maui, Texas or any other sweet onions, too.

MAKES 4 TO 6 SERVINGS

1 medium sweet onion

4 tablespoons vegetable oil

2 teaspoons bacon drippings (optional)

1 cup self-rising corn bread mix

1¼ cups whole milk, plus more as needed

1 large egg

1. Preheat the oven to 425°F.
2. Peel the onion, cut off the top and bottom ends, and slice it into circles of uniform thickness. Finely chop the tops and bottoms and reserve them in a small bowl.
3. Pour 3 tablespoons of the oil into a well-seasoned 9-inch cast-iron skillet over medium heat. Add the bacon drippings, if using. Once the oil begins to ripple, add the onion slices to the skillet in a single layer. Cook, adjusting the heat as necessary, for 4 minutes, or until the onion slices are lightly caramelized on the bottom. Using a spatula, flip the onions over and cook for 1 minute more. Remove the pan from the heat, leaving the onions in place.
4. Place the corn bread mix in a large mixing bowl and add the reserved chopped onion tops and bottoms. Thoroughly whisk together the milk, the egg, and the remaining 1 tablespoon of the oil in a separate mixing bowl. Make a well in the dry ingredient mixture, pour in the buttermilk mixture, and stir until just combined. If necessary to make the batter pourable, add a little more milk.
5. Return the hot skillet to medium heat. When the onion slices begin to sizzle, pour in the batter (it should sizzle as well). Carefully place the skillet in the oven and bake for 25 to 35 minutes, or until the corn bread is golden brown on top. Remove from the oven and set aside to cool for 5 minutes.
6. Carefully invert the skillet over a serving plate; the corn bread should drop right out. Serve warm.

Spoon Bread

A Southern favorite, spoon bread is really a cornmeal pudding. It is eaten as a side dish and may appear at any meal. Boiling the cornmeal briefly with milk causes it to absorb more moisture, producing a smooth, creamy consistency. Be sure to use meal that's labeled "stone ground" as it retains all of the components of whole-grain corn, which is essential for the flavor of this dish.

MAKES 4 TO 6 SERVINGS

1 cup stone-ground cornmeal

3 cups whole milk

3 large eggs, well beaten

3 teaspoons baking powder

1 teaspoon salt

1 tablespoon unsalted butter, melted

1. Preheat the oven to 350°F. Grease a 9-by-5-inch or larger rectangular baking dish.

2. Stir the cornmeal into 2 cups of the milk in a large saucepan. Place the saucepan over medium heat and, while stirring constantly, bring the mixture to a boil.

3. Once the mixture has thickened, remove from the heat and stir in the remaining milk, followed by the eggs, baking powder, salt, and butter.

4. Scrape the batter into the prepared baking dish and bake for 30 minutes, or until the center is set and the edges are beginning to brown. Remove from the oven and set aside to cool for 10 minutes (it will firm up as it cools).

5. Serve warm.

Cornmeal Mush (Polenta) Cakes

Cornmeal mush is hard to beat for versatility. Served hot, it can take the place of rice, grits, or pasta; it's also a welcome foil for rich gravies and sauces. Chilling renders it solid enough to cut with a knife, and the slices can be fried or baked—opening up pairing possibilities with meat, fowl, or fish. Cold polenta keeps for several days in the refrigerator, too.

MAKES 8 SIDE-DISH SERVINGS (APPROXIMATELY 4 CUPS)

8 cups water

Salt

3 cups stone-ground yellow cornmeal

Vegetable oil, for frying

All-purpose flour, for coating

Note: To make smaller amounts of cornmeal mush, the proper quantities are 2⅔ cups water to 1 cup cornmeal or 1⅓ cups water to ½ cup cornmeal.

1. Place the water in a large saucepan over medium heat and bring it almost to a boil. Add a pinch of the salt. Sprinkle in the cornmeal, letting it sift through your fingers like sand (if the water is hot but not quite boiling, this technique will result in few, if any, lumps). Stir, raise the heat to medium-high, and, stirring constantly, bring to a slow simmer. Cook, stirring constantly, for about 10 minutes, or until the mixture is smooth and creamy. Remove from the heat, taste, and add more of the salt as needed.

2. Serve immediately, if using warm.

3. To slice and fry the cornmeal mush: Pour the cooked mush into a shallow pan and set aside to cool to room temperature.

4. Refrigerate overnight; the mush will become firm enough to be sliced into bars or cut into rounds using a biscuit cutter.

5. Pour enough oil into a heavy skillet to coat the bottom well and place it over medium heat. Warm the oil until it ripples and a light haze forms over it.

6. Lightly coat each of the pieces of firm mush with the flour. Add the pieces, a few at a time, to the hot skillet and cook, turning once, for approximately 3 minutes per side or until browned.

7. Serve warm.

Succotash

According to legend, the name of this Native American dish translates to "broken corn kernels." It's a flavorsome combination of vegetables, all of which come into season at the same time. You can also make it in winter using frozen vegetables.

MAKES 4 SIDE-DISH SERVINGS

2 tablespoons olive oil

½ cup chopped red onion

1 cup baby lima beans, frozen and thawed or fresh and blanched

1 cup corn kernels, fresh or frozen and thawed

1 cup diced summer squash

1 cup vegetable stock

4 fresh thyme sprigs

Salt

Freshly ground black pepper

1. Warm the oil in a small skillet over medium-high heat. Add the onion and cook gently, stirring once or twice, for about 2 minutes, or until softened. Add the remaining vegetables and cook, stirring occasionally, for about 2 minutes, or until the onion is translucent.

2. Pour the vegetable stock into the skillet. Add the thyme, a pinch of the salt, and a few grinds of the black pepper. Reduce the heat to medium-low and simmer for 10 minutes, or until the beans are tender. Remove from the heat and cover to keep warm until you are ready to serve.

3. Serve warm.

Hominy with Summer Vegetables

Inspired by succotash, this quick stir-fry of vegetables with canned hominy captures the abundance of late summer in the Appalachian foothills. This dish would be great with my Meatloaf with Wild Mushrooms (page 102).

MAKES 4 TO 6 SIDE-DISH SERVINGS

1 tablespoon vegetable oil

1 small red onion, chopped

1 medium red bell pepper, stemmed, seeded, and chopped

1 medium zucchini, diced

½ teaspoon chili powder

½ teaspoon dried oregano

1 cup baby lima beans, frozen and thawed

1 cup canned hominy, drained and liquid reserved

1 teaspoon red wine vinegar

Salt

Freshly ground black pepper

Chopped fresh tomatoes, for garnish

Chopped fresh flat-leaf parsley, for garnish

Chopped fresh cilantro, for garnish

1. Warm the oil in a large skillet with a lid over medium heat. Add the onion and cook, stirring occasionally, until softened. Add the bell pepper, zucchini, chili powder, and oregano and cook, stirring often, until the onion is translucent. Add the lima beans, the hominy, and a tablespoon or two of the hominy liquid.

2. Reduce the heat to medium-low, cover, and simmer for 15 minutes, or until the lima beans are tender. Remove from the heat and stir in the vinegar. Season to taste with the salt and black pepper.

3. Serve garnished with the tomatoes, parsley, and cilantro.

NIXTAMALIZATION

Centuries ago, the indigenous people of Mesoamerica discovered the process of nixtamalization. Ripe corn is freed of its tough outer seed coat by soaking it in a hot solution of lye, which is made by combining water with wood ashes and straining out the solids. Very likely, the corn was mixed with the lye solution in a large pottery vessel and then cooked over a slow fire until the seed coats could easily be removed from the grains by hand.

Corn kernels treated this way become what we call "hominy." Besides removing the corn's tough coat and rendering it more palatable, nixtamalization also chemically alters the corn's niacin, making it more biologically available to humans. This benefit improved corn's nutritional value and it thus became a staple food; without a doubt, it contributed to the rise of ancient civilizations.

The technique migrated from Mesoamerica to the southwestern United States and eventually appeared in the southern Appalachians along with the Mississippian culture, which thrived there from about the first century until the late seventeenth century.

Hominy can be found in cans in most grocery stores throughout the region, while Latino markets stock *posole*, hominy that has been re-dried to improve its storage life. Coarsely ground posole, known as "hominy grits," has now been largely replaced by whole-grain corn grits; *masa harina* is posole that's as finely ground as wheat flour.

Sweet Corn on the Cob

Sweet corn is one of the pleasures of summer—all the more so if it's homegrown. Modern hybrid sweet corns have enormous amounts of sugar and mutations in their enzymes that convert sugar to starch (see facing page). This results in a long shelf life after picking, but the cost is that old-fashioned "corny" flavor. If you can locate normal-sugar corn varieties at the farmers' market, or grow your own, you can enjoy a true southern Appalachian treat. Just be sure to pick the corn when it is ripe and cook it the same day.

MAKES 4 SIDE-DISH SERVINGS

4 fresh-picked sweet corn ears

Butter

Salt

Freshly ground black pepper

Note: Apply some hot sauce to the corn, if that's your preference, before or after cooking.

1. Carefully pull back the corn husks and remove as much of the silk as possible. Trim off the pointed end of the cob with a sharp knife. Pull the husks back over the ears, enclosing them. (The corn ears can be prepared up to this point several hours in advance; if doing so, store them in the refrigerator and bring to room temperature before proceeding with the recipe.)

2. Preheat the oven to 350°F. Submerge each ear in a large bowl filled with cold water. Allow the ears to drain briefly and then place them directly on the rack of the hot oven. Bake for 30 minutes. (Test for doneness using a pair of tongs; the ears should give a little when squeezed.)

3. Remove from the oven and serve immediately with the butter, salt, and black pepper.

SWEET CORN VARIETIES

Once upon a time, the conventional wisdom said to start the water boiling before heading out to the garden patch to harvest some fresh sweet corn. It was well known that corn begins to lose sweetness from the moment of harvest, and the goal of the cook was to preserve as much of that sweet taste as possible. Most traditional corn varieties are only sweet for 3 to 5 days.

Enter the plant breeders, who have now given us corn with kernels that are up to 50 percent sugar. This corn remains sweet for days after harvest, permitting it to be shipped long distances. These "super sweet" and "enhanced sugar" corn hybrids also appear at farmers' markets. Names like "Ambrosia," "Peaches and Cream," and "Honey and Pearl" denote just how sweet they are.

The downside is a loss of traditional corn flavor components that give corn its special taste. If you want that traditional flavor, find someone in your area who grows Silver Queen, Golden Bantam, or Iochief—all traditional sweet corn varieties that have been around for decades.

Corn Pudding

To get this right, it is essential that the corn be scraped, not cut, from the cob. Use an extra-large bowl to catch splatters. Holding each cob by the pointed end, use the dull side of a knife to scrape as much corn and juice from the cob as possible. The result should look like corn kernels mixed with ricotta or cottage cheese.

MAKES 6 SIDE-DISH SERVINGS

2 tablespoons unsalted butter

4 cups fresh summer corn, scraped from the cobs (about 6 ears)

Freshly ground white pepper

¾ cup heavy whipping cream

1. Preheat the oven to 350°F. Use some of the butter to grease a casserole dish generously.

2. Place the corn in the dish and smooth it into an even layer (without packing it in). Dot the top with the remaining butter and several grinds of the white pepper. Drizzle the cream over the top and bake at 350°F for 1 hour, or until golden and bubbly.

3. Remove from the oven and serve hot.

Corn Chowder

A comforting way to use fresh corn, this recipe is best when the corn is fresh and summer is at its height.

MAKES 4 SERVINGS

2 to 3 fresh corn ears

¾ teaspoon ground paprika

½ teaspoon garlic powder

½ teaspoon mustard powder

½ teaspoon freshly ground black pepper

¼ teaspoon white pepper

¼ teaspoon dried thyme

¼ teaspoon dried basil

½ teaspoon salt

½ cup water

¼ cup dry white wine

2 cups vegetable stock

2 tablespoons olive oil

¾ cup chopped onion

¾ cup chopped bell pepper (any color)

¾ cup chopped celery

1 cup vegetable stock

2 tablespoons chopped fresh cilantro, for garnish

¼ cup freshly grated Manchego or Cheddar, for garnish

1. Cut the kernels from the corn and reserve the cobs (this should yield about 1 cup of kernels).
2. Combine the paprika, garlic powder, mustard powder, black pepper, white pepper, thyme, basil, and salt in a small bowl and set aside.
3. Combine the corn kernels and the water in a saucepan over medium-high heat and bring to a boil. Reduce the heat to medium-low and simmer for 5 minutes. Remove from the heat. Drain the kernels into a colander over a bowl and reserve the drained liquid.
4. Combine the reserved corn liquid and corn cobs, the wine, and 1 cup of the vegetable stock in a medium saucepan over medium heat and bring to a boil. Reduce the heat to medium-low and simmer for 30 minutes.
5. Heat the oil in another medium saucepan over medium heat and sauté the onion until translucent. Add half of the spice mixture, the bell pepper, and the celery and sauté until the onion is golden.
6. To the onion mixture, add the corn kernels, the remaining 1 cup of vegetable stock, the remaining spice mixture, and the corn stock (discard the cobs) and simmer for 10 minutes. Remove from the heat.
7. Serve hot garnished with the cilantro and cheese.

Soup Beans

My grandmother made beans every day and served them at both lunch and dinner (or, as we say around here, "dinner and supper.") They were always served with corn bread and lots of seasonal vegetables—sometimes even green beans. Good-quality dried pinto beans are easy to find, and with a few simple touches, you can re-create the flavor of Grandma's recipe. Beans should be soaked overnight prior to cooking. If you don't have time for the overnight soak, cover the beans with cold water to a depth of 1 inch in a medium saucepan over high heat and bring to a boil. Boil for 1 minute and then remove from the heat. Cover tightly and allow to sit for 1 hour. Drain and proceed to cook as directed in the recipe.

MAKES 4 SIDE-DISH SERVINGS OR 2 AS A MAIN DISH

1 cup dried pinto beans

2 garlic cloves, peeled

1 bay leaf

1 fresh thyme sprig

3 black peppercorns

Salt

1. Rinse the beans a time or two; pick over them and discard any pebbles or other foreign matter. Place the beans in a suitable container with enough water to cover them by 1 inch and refrigerate overnight.

2. Drain the beans and transfer them to a medium saucepan. Add enough cold water to cover them by 1 inch and add the garlic to the pan.

3. Wrap the bay leaf, thyme, and peppercorns in a small square of cheesecloth and tie it with kitchen string, making a *bouquet garni* that can be removed easily. Add the *bouquet garni* to the pan but do not salt the beans until they are cooked.

4. Place the saucepan over medium heat and slowly bring to a steady boil. Reduce the heat to medium-low, cover, and cook, adding hot water periodically to prevent the beans from getting too dry and stirring from time to time, for 1½ to 2 hours, or until the beans are tender. As they cook, check frequently;

if a few beans burn at the bottom, the whole pot is ruined. Test for doneness by mashing a bean against the side of the pot with the back of a spoon; there should be little resistance. Remove and discard the *bouquet garni*. Taste for seasoning and add as much salt as you deem appropriate. Reduce the heat to low to keep hot until ready to serve.

Notes: Some cooks like to mash the 2 cloves of garlic, along with some of the beans, with a potato masher, creating a "soupier" dish. This is purely a matter of personal preference.

This recipe is vegan, but few seasonings work better with beans than bacon, so feel free to add a chopped slice or two.

Shuck Beans with Bacon

Leather Britches (page 25) are also called "shuck beans," in reference to their pods, or "shucks," that are cooked along with the bean seeds. Leather britches are simple to make at home, and so is this recipe. The first boiling removes dust and other contaminants that may have accumulated on the beans during the drying process (you can omit this step if your beans were dried in a dehydrator). Benton's bacon (see Sources, page 183) will make this dish extra-special.

MAKES 4 SIDE-DISH SERVINGS

3 cups Leather Britches (page 25), stem ends removed

3 strips bacon, chopped

Pinch of sugar

Freshly ground black pepper

1. Place the beans in a large saucepan or Dutch oven with a lid. Cover them with water and place the pan over high heat. When the water comes to a boil, reduce the heat to medium-low and simmer for 1 minute. Remove from the heat. Drain the beans into a colander and return them to the saucepan.

2. Add the bacon, the sugar, a few grinds of the black pepper, and enough water to cover the beans by 1 inch. Place the pot over medium-high heat and bring to a boil.

3. Reduce the heat to medium-low, cover, and simmer until the beans are meltingly tender (this may take 1 hour or more; test by carefully biting into a bean). When the beans are done, keep them warm on the back of the stove until time to serve.

Baked Beans

This recipe is a labor of love. I've been trying to replicate my mother's baked beans, a dish she frequently took to church suppers and on picnics, for years, and this comes as close as I have been able to manage. I use homemade tomato ketchup, but any good organic product should give the same results. If you lack the time to make Homemade Beer Mustard (page 16), use any good coarse-grained mustard. The recipe can be easily doubled. It can also be made with 2 cups of cooked navy beans prepared from ½ cup of dry beans. Soak the dry beans overnight in water to cover by 1 inch. Drain and place them in a large saucepan. Cover again with water and cook at a gentle boil for 1 hour, or until the beans are tender but not falling apart. Test by mashing a bean against the side of the pot with a spoon. If it yields easily, remove from the heat.

MAKES 4 SIDE-DISH SERVINGS

One 15-ounce can navy beans

½ cup chopped sweet onion

¼ cup plus 2 tablespoons ketchup

2 tablespoons dark brown sugar, densely packed

2 tablespoons unsulphured molasses

1½ teaspoons Worcestershire sauce

½ teaspoon Homemade Beer Mustard (page 16)

¼ teaspoon garlic powder

1. Preheat the oven to 300°F.
2. Drain the beans into a colander positioned over a bowl and reserve the liquid.
3. Combine the beans, all of the remaining ingredients, and enough of the reserved bean liquid to cover the beans by ¼ inch in a 1½-quart baking dish. Bake for 45 minutes to 1 hour, or until bubbly and reduced. Remove from the oven and serve hot, warm, or at room temperature.

Note: The beans can be garnished with chopped cooked bacon, if you like.

Green Beans and Taters

Combining these two vegetables in the same pot probably came about because the first potatoes and green beans are ready to harvest at the same time, when the days are warm and the weather is settled. This time comes earlier or later depending upon how high up in the mountains your garden grows. The recipe makes equally good sense in winter, when canned or dried green beans and stored potatoes—flavored with cured pork—make satisfying comfort food. I like to serve this recipe at Thanksgiving instead of the ubiquitous green bean casserole. I prefer a low-starch potato variety, such as Red Pontiac or Yukon Gold, but use whatever potatoes look best in the market.

MAKES 4 SIDE-DISH SERVINGS

3 ounces country ham, chopped

1 teaspoon bacon drippings

1 garlic clove, chopped

1 quart canned green beans (preferably homemade)

3 medium potatoes

Salt

Freshly ground black pepper

1. Warm the bacon drippings in a large saucepan over medium heat. Add the ham and cook, stirring occasionally, until it begins to brown. Stir in the garlic and cook for 1 minute. Add the beans and their liquid and bring to a simmer. Cover and cook over low heat for 5 minutes while you prepare the potatoes.

2. Peel the potatoes and cut them into uniform chunks no larger than an egg; uniformity means the potatoes will cook evenly. Rinse the potatoes under cold running water to remove excess starch. Drain the potatoes thoroughly and then add them to the pot with the beans, making sure to tuck them under the surface. Increase the heat to medium. When the water returns to a simmer, reduce the heat to medium-low, cover, and cook for 20 minutes, or until the potatoes are done. To determine doneness, pierce 1 potato with a bamboo skewer, if it meets no resistance, they're done.

3. Taste for seasoning and add the salt and black pepper as you deem appropriate. Keep warm until you are ready to serve.

4. Serve warm.

Speckled Butter Beans

This lima bean has a long history in the South. Apparently, several heirloom varieties date back to colonial times, with different strains of the seeds being saved in different locations. Like all lima beans, these prefer warmth. They are thus not often grown in the higher elevations of the southern Appalachians. They are available frozen, or you can find fresh ones in the farmers' market in late summer. About 2½ pounds of unshelled beans will yield 1 pound of shelled ones.

MAKES 4 TO 6 SIDE-DISH SERVINGS

2 cups water, plus more as needed

2 cups chicken stock

1 small white onion, chopped

¼ green bell pepper, seeded and chopped

2 ounces smoked bacon or fatback, chopped

1 garlic clove, minced

1 bay leaf

1 fresh thyme sprig

1 pound shelled fresh speckled butter beans

1 cup chopped canned tomatoes, drained

Salt

Freshly ground black pepper

4 scallions sliced thinly on the diagonal, for garnish

1. Combine the water, chicken stock, onion, bell pepper, bacon, garlic, bay leaf, and thyme in a large saucepan or Dutch oven over high heat and bring to a rolling boil. Reduce the heat to medium and simmer, partially covered, for 15 minutes. Add more water as needed if the stock becomes too reduced.

2. Add the butter beans and enough water to cover them by ½ inch. Bring to a simmer and then reduce the heat to low. Simmer gently, covered, until the beans are tender but not falling apart, about 20 minutes.

3. Stir in the tomatoes and remove from the heat. Taste for seasoning and add the salt and black pepper as needed.

4. Serve the beans with as much or as little of the liquid as you like; garnish with the chopped scallions.

Warm Bean Salad in Roasted Sweet Onions

The most famous Southern sweet onions come from Vidalia, Georgia, and these days, they're widely available (this type of onion does not grow well in Tennessee and North Carolina). Various types of red summer onions are also sweet enough for this recipe. They start showing up in farmers' markets in July, about a month after the Vidalia onions. At other times of the year, sweet onions come from Texas and Hawaii. Chop up the tops and insides of the onions and use them to make Onion Jam (page 27). The White Acre peas included in the bean salad are one of many varieties of field peas grown throughout the South. If you can't find them, substitute navy beans.

MAKES 6 SIDE-DISH SERVINGS, WITH LEFTOVERS

FOR THE SALAD:

6 medium sweet onions, each about 4 inches in diameter, peeled

1½ cups green beans, frozen and thawed (see Note)

Salt

One 15-ounce can White Acre field peas, drained and rinsed

One 15-ounce can red kidney or pinto beans, drained and rinsed

1 small red bell pepper, stemmed, seeded, and finely diced

1 small hot red pepper, stemmed, seeded, and thinly sliced (optional)

FOR THE DRESSING:

6 bacon slices, cut into 1-inch pieces

3 tablespoons apple cider vinegar

3 tablespoons water

3 tablespoons light brown sugar

1½ teaspoons dried oregano

¾ teaspoon salt

Freshly ground black pepper

Vegetable oil, as needed

3 scallions, white and green parts, thinly sliced on the diagonal

1. Prepare the salad: Preheat the oven to 375°F. If necessary to make them sit upright, remove a thin slice from the bottom of each onion. Place the onions in a baking dish that is large enough to hold them in one layer and add enough water to come halfway up the sides of the onions. Bake for 1½ hours.

2. Using tongs, carefully invert the onions and bake for 1½ hours. Remove from the oven. Using tongs, place the onions on a rack over a sheet pan to drain and cool. Discard the water in the baking dish and set aside the onions to cool to room temperature. (The onions can be prepared up to this point 1 day in advance; if doing so, store them, covered,

in the refrigerator and bring to room temperature before proceeding with the recipe.)

3. Place the green beans in a stockpot and cover them with water. Salt the water and place the stockpot over medium heat. Bring to a simmer and cook until the beans are tender, 8 to 10 minutes. Remove from the heat, drain, and place in a large, heatproof bowl. Add the White Acre peas, the kidney beans, the bell pepper, and the hot pepper, if using.

4. Preheat the oven to 200°F. Remove the outer layers from the onions and discard them. Slice off the tops of the onions and reserve the tops. Carefully spoon the inside of the onions out, leaving only two or three outer layers that form a cup. (Use the inside layers and the tops for another recipe.)

5. Stir the bean mixture until well combined and then fill each of the onion cups with the mixture, mounding each slightly on top (there will be leftover bean salad; see Note). Set the filled onion cups in heatproof individual serving bowls and place them in the oven to keep warm while you make the dressing.

6. Prepare the dressing: Cook the bacon in a small saucepan over medium heat until it is crisp and has rendered its fat.

7. While the bacon cooks, combine the vinegar, the water, the brown sugar, the oregano, the salt, and a few grinds of the black pepper in a small bowl. Stir until the sugar and salt have dissolved.

8. When the bacon is done, remove from the heat. Remove it from the saucepan with a slotted spoon and set aside on a plate lined with paper towels to drain.

9. The saucepan should contain 2 tablespoons of drippings; if not, add enough vegetable oil to make up the difference. Reduce the heat to medium-low and stir the vinegar mixture into the saucepan. While stirring the mixture constantly, bring to a boil. Remove from the heat.

10. Remove the onions from the oven and pour equal portions of the hot dressing over them. Garnish with the scallions and the reserved bacon pieces.

11. Serve immediately.

Notes: If you prefer to use fresh green beans, increase the cooking time to 10 to 12 minutes in step 3.

Store the leftover bean salad, covered, in the refrigerator for up to 3 days. Bring the leftovers to room temperature and mix with the dressing from this recipe or your favorite vinaigrette and some chopped scallions to serve as a side dish.

FRENCH BEANS

Green beans are as ubiquitous as bacon in the kitchens of southern Appalachia. Whether dried into leather britches, canned, or pickled, green beans are a pantry staple. Less commonly used are the slender, sweet beans known in France as *haricots verts*. These "French beans," as we call them, are not (as commonly supposed) merely younger specimens of typical green beans. These are beans specifically bred to produce their delicious pods in flushes from mid- to late summer. Typically harvested when they are about 6 inches in length and ³⁄₁₆ inch in diameter, French beans do not freeze or can well, but they do make passable pickles. They are at their best when freshly harvested, lightly steamed, and served as a side dish along with other seasonal vegetables.

Your best bet is to grow them yourself. Beans are notoriously simple to grow. You can produce four to six servings of French beans grown in a simple oblong planter about 30 inches long.

French Bean and Sweet Corn Salad

Several of summer's greatest garden delicacies combine in this light, refreshing, fat-free salad. The recipe can be easily multiplied to serve additional guests. French beans, or *haricots verts*, are bred specially to be tender and sweet. If you cannot find them, substitute any thin green bean and increase the time in the boiling water to 6 minutes.

MAKES 4 SIDE-DISH SERVINGS

2 corn ears

1 pound French green beans, each about 5 inches long

⅓ cup chopped red onion

¼ cup chopped red sweet pepper

1 tablespoon torn fresh basil leaves

2 teaspoons rice vinegar

Salt

Freshly ground black pepper

1. Bring a large pot of water over high heat to a boil. Drop in the corn ear and cook for 3 minutes. Remove the ear with a slotted spoon and transfer it to a bowl of cold water to stop the cooking process. Remove the ear, drain, and cut the kernels from the ear with a sharp knife. Discard the cob and place the kernels in a bowl.

2. Return the water to a boil. Drop in the beans and cook for 2 minutes. Drain the beans into a colander and refresh them under cold running water. Place the beans on kitchen towels to drain.

3. Trim the beans' stems, cut them into ¾-inch pieces, and add them to the bowl containing the corn kernels.

4. Add the onion, sweet pepper, basil, and vinegar to the bowl and season with the salt and black pepper. Toss until well combined. Refrigerate for 1 hour and up to 3 days before serving.

5. Serve cold.

Hoppin' John

No one seems to know whence came the name for this traditional dish of black-eyed peas and rice.

MAKES 4 SIDE-DISH SERVINGS

1 tablespoon bacon drippings

½ cup chopped onion

1 garlic clove, minced

¾ teaspoon fresh or ¼ teaspoon dried oregano

One 15-ounce can black-eyed peas, drained

1½ cups hot cooked rice

Chopped fresh scallions, for garnish

Hot sauce (optional)

1. Warm the bacon drippings in a large skillet over medium heat. Add the onion and cook until it is translucent.

2. Add the garlic, oregano, and peas to the skillet. Cover and cook for 10 minutes. Remove from the heat and stir the rice into the mixture.

3. Serve immediately, garnished with the scallions and the hot sauce, if desired.

Stuffed Zucchini

Filling vegetables with savory stuffing is a kitchen technique with a long history. This recipe brings the flavors of the mountain South to an Italian classic.

MAKES 4 TO 8 SIDE-DISH SERVINGS

4 medium zucchinis

1 pound ground pork

1 teaspoon garlic powder

1 teaspoon onion powder

1 teaspoon ground smoked Spanish paprika

1 teaspoon salt

½ teaspoon freshly ground black pepper

¼ teaspoon ground cayenne pepper

2 tablespoons bacon drippings

1 cup chopped onion

¾ cup chopped celery

¾ cup chopped green bell pepper

1 cup corn bread crumbs

1 cup freshly grated white Cheddar

1 large egg, well beaten

1. Preheat the oven to 300°F. Grease a large baking dish.

2. Slice the zucchini in half lengthwise. Using a melon baller, carefully remove most of the pulp of each half, leaving shells about ¼ inch thick. Arrange the shells in the prepared baking dish and chop up and reserve the pulp.

3. Combine the pork, garlic powder, onion powder, paprika, salt, black pepper, and cayenne pepper in a large mixing bowl and, using your hands, mix until well combined.

4. Warm the bacon drippings in a large, heavy skillet over medium heat. Add the pork and cook, turning often and breaking it up with a spatula, until no more pink remains. Using a slotted spoon, transfer the pork to a clean mixing bowl and drain off all but 1 tablespoon of the fat remaining in the skillet.

5. Add the onion, celery, bell pepper, and reserved zucchini pulp to the skillet and cook, stirring constantly, for 4 minutes, or until the onion is translucent. Remove from the heat.

6. Transfer the cooked vegetables to the bowl containing the pork and add the corn bread crumbs, cheese, and egg. Stir until well combined.

7. Stuff the zucchini shells with the mixture and return them to the baking dish. Bake for 1 hour. Remove from the oven.

8. Serve hot.

Summer Squash Casserole

Church suppers and family reunions in the southern Appalachian region almost always have some version of this casserole. This one gets a flavor punch from roasting the squash. Make it with zucchini, yellow crookneck, or pattypan squash, or use a combination.

MAKES 6 SIDE-DISH SERVINGS

1 tablespoon olive oil

2 pounds summer squash

1 medium onion

Salt

Freshly ground black pepper

2 sleeves saltine crackers

4 tablespoons (½ stick) unsalted butter, melted

4 medium carrots

6 tablespoons (¾ stick) unsalted butter, room temperature

2 tablespoons all-purpose flour

1¾ cups chicken stock

¼ teaspoon dried thyme leaves

8 ounces sour cream

1.　Preheat the oven to 350°F. Line a sheet pan with aluminum foil and drizzle it with a little of the oil.

2.　Trim and cut the squash into ¼-inch-thick slices and slice the onion into ¼-inch rounds. Spread the vegetables on the sheet pan in a single layer. Drizzle the remainder of the oil over the vegetables and sprinkle them with the salt and black pepper. Bake for 10 minutes.

3.　Using tongs, turn the vegetables and bake for an additional 10 to 15 minutes, or until the squash is lightly browned. Remove from the oven and reduce the temperature to 325°F.

4.　Crush 1 sleeve of the crackers and combine them with the melted butter in a mixing bowl. Line the bottom of a large casserole dish with the mixture and set aside.

5. Shred the carrots using the largest holes of a box grater.

6. Melt 2 tablespoons of the room-temperature butter in a medium saucepan over medium-low heat. Make a roux by adding the flour and cooking, stirring constantly, for 1 minute. While stirring constantly, add the chicken stock in a steady stream. Add the thyme.

7. Raise the heat to medium and simmer the mixture for 3 minutes. Taste for seasoning and add the salt and black pepper as needed.

8. Add the carrots to the saucepan and stir in the sour cream. Last, stir in the roasted vegetables and remove from the heat. Pour the mixture into the prepared casserole dish.

9. Crush the remaining sleeve of saltines and spread them on top of the casserole. Dot with the remaining 4 tablespoons of butter. Bake for 30 to 40 minutes, or until lightly browned on top and bubbly at the edges. Remove from the oven.

10. Serve hot.

Squash Blossoms Stuffed with Ricotta

Squash blossoms are a fleeting, seasonal treat so perishable that you're unlikely to find them unless you request them at a farmers' market. Look for the vendor who offers the largest selection of summer squashes. While the male blossoms are tasty, female ones with a little squash at the bottom are even better.

MAKES 2 SIDE-DISH SERVINGS

6 squash blossoms

1 cup whole-milk ricotta

1 tablespoon torn fresh basil leaves

Salt

Freshly ground black pepper

¾ cup chilled club soda

½ cup brown rice flour

1 teaspoon cornstarch

2 cups peanut oil, for deep frying

1. Carefully rinse the blossoms in cool water. Remove and discard the floral parts from the interior of each blossom and set the blossoms aside on a tray lined with paper towels.

2. Combine the ricotta and basil in a small bowl and season with the salt and black pepper to taste. Transfer the mixture to a pastry bag fitted with a plain tip or a zip-top plastic bag and refrigerate.

3. Combine the club soda, flour, and cornstarch in a large mixing bowl and whisk until well combined and a batter forms.

4. Warm the oil to 350°F in a large, heavy-bottom saucepan or deep fryer. One at a time, dip the squash blossoms into the batter, allowing any excess to drain back into the bowl. Drop each blossom into the hot oil and fry for 15 to 20 seconds, or until the batter has set. Remove the blossoms to a plate lined with paper towels to drain. Repeat until all of the blossoms have been fried and remove from the heat.

5. When all of the blossoms have been cooked, carefully pipe equal portions of the ricotta mixture into each one. If you are not using a pastry bag, slice off one of the bottom

corners of the plastic bag and force the mixture through the open corner into the blossoms. As you fill each blossom, place it on an individual serving plate.

6. Serve immediately.

Note: Any leftover ricotta mixture can be stored in a covered container in the refrigerator for up to 3 days. Use it to dress up raw summer vegetables, such as zucchini, yellow squash, tomatoes, or fresh corn.

Winter Squash Soup

Winter squash often stands in for sweet potatoes, and vice versa. Either is enhanced by warm spice and smoky flavors, which come together in this comforting soup. I prefer acorn squash for this soup, but you can use any winter squash that looks good. Squash vary in size from the little delicata and acorn types to larger butternuts to enormous cushaws you may see at the farmers' market. For this recipe, you will need only 1 cup of roasted squash, so a small squash specimen will suffice.

MAKES 4 FIRST-COURSE SERVINGS

Oil for brushing the squash

1 small to medium winter squash

1 tablespoon vegetable oil

1 medium onion, chopped

1 garlic clove, minced

2 cups chicken or vegetable stock, plus more as needed

1 teaspoon minced crystallized ginger

1 tablespoon red miso

½ teaspoon smoked Spanish paprika

¼ teaspoon ground cinnamon

Hot sauce, as desired

Water (optional)

Toasted Pepitas or Squash Seeds (page 68), for garnish

1. Preheat the oven to 400°F. Line a 9-by-13-inch baking pan with aluminum foil.

2. Cut the squash in half lengthwise and scoop out the seeds (see Note). Brush the cut sides of the squash with the oil and place the halves, cut side down, in the baking pan. Roast until the skin begins to brown and the flesh is tender when pierced with the tip of a knife; start checking after 20 minutes, but the exact baking time will depend on the age and size of the squash. Remove from the oven and set aside until the squash is cool enough to handle.

3. Scrape the flesh from the skin into a bowl and discard the skin. Add any pan juices to the bowl containing the squash and set aside.

4. Warm the oil in a large saucepan over medium heat until the oil ripples. Add the onion and cook, stirring occasionally, until it is translucent. Add the garlic and continue cooking, stirring frequently, for 1 minute. Add the reserved squash, chicken stock, and ginger and bring to a boil. Reduce the heat to medium-low and simmer 15 minutes.

5. Place the miso in a small ladle and, while holding it in the saucepan with one hand, stir with a second spoon in the other hand until it is fully incorporated into the soup. (Just tossing it in will produce lumps.) Add the paprika, cinnamon, and as much hot sauce as you like. Taste for seasoning and adjust as needed. Remove from the heat and set aside to cool for 30 minutes.

6. Transfer the soup to a blender and puree (in batches, if necessary). (You can also puree the soup in the saucepan using an immersion blender.)

7. Return the pureed soup to the saucepan over low heat and warm through. Remove from the heat. If the soup seems too thick, thin it with water or stock to the consistency you prefer.

8. Ladle the soup into serving bowls and serve garnished with the toasted pepitas.

Note: Save the squash seeds and wash them thoroughly in a colander to remove any stringy flesh. The seeds of some types of squash are easier to separate than others. It's not necessary to get every trace of the flesh, but removing it keeps the seeds from sticking together when toasted. Spread them out on kitchen towels to dry. See page 68 for instructions for toasting seeds.

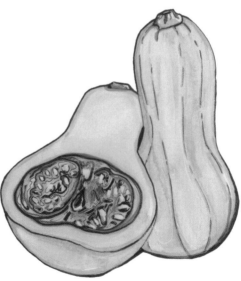

Toasted Pepitas or Squash Seeds

Toasting seeds brings out their nutty flavor. Use them to garnish soups or salads, or as a snack.

SERVINGS VARY

Raw pepitas (pumpkin seeds) or seeds from a medium winter squash, washed and dried

Salt (optional)

Place the seeds in a dry skillet over medium-high heat. Cook, shaking the skillet from time to time. When several seeds have popped and many are lightly browned, remove from the heat and transfer the seeds into a metal bowl. Add the salt while the seeds are hot, if desired.

CRUZE FARM

Out on the east side of Knox County, Tennessee, generations of the Cruze family have been managing a fine herd of Jersey cows. Jersey milk is renowned for its high butterfat and protein content, and its flavor must be experienced to be fully appreciated. Besides whole milk, the farm produces ice cream, butter, buttermilk, and low-fat milk. A conservation easement on the land ensures that Cruze Farm will remain a farm for generations to come. Many Knoxville chefs rely on Cruze Farm dairy products to make creamy ricotta and buttery pastries, among other creations.

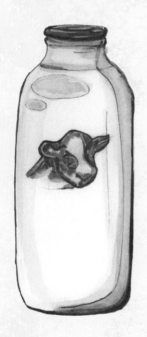

Chapter Three

TATERS, MATERS, AND MORE

People are often surprised to learn that many foods commonly consumed today were completely unknown in Europe prior to the European discovery of North America. "Irish" potatoes, for example, are native to Peru.

On the other hand, cabbage and all of the other members of the radish family, including radishes, turnips, rutabaga, mustards, broccoli, kale, cauliflower, kohlrabi, and Brussels sprouts—as well as asparagus, carrots, and cereal grains—were unknown to Native Americans prior to the Europeans' arrival. By great good fortune, these European vegetables have thrived in the rich soils and mild climate of the southern Appalachians.

Further, the influence of enslaved people of African descent on Southern cooking in general cannot be overestimated. They brought with them okra, peanuts, sweet potatoes, and sorghum.

As a consequence of this abundance, we have a long tradition here in Appalachia of putting out enormous spreads of multiple vegetable dishes—especially at the height of the summer season. Traditionally, the rationale was that if God allowed all these vegetables to mature at the same time, He must have meant for us to eat them together.

Corn Bread Salad

The origin of corn bread salad is something of a mystery. Could it be that Appalachian cooks, who often served cold corn bread and buttermilk for their family's evening meal, decided to add fresh garden vegetables to the dish? I note that modern versions of the salad often include ranch dressing—of which buttermilk is a well-known ingredient. This version gets its tang from blue cheese, rather than buttermilk. Feel free to add or substitute other seasonal vegetables, and to increase the proportion of corn bread as you see fit. Make this recipe with Easy Corn Bread (page 34) or Heirloom Corn Bread (page 35). Half of a 9-inch skillet is the amount of corn bread I typically have left over.

MAKES 4 SIDE-DISH SERVINGS

FOR THE SALAD:

Leftover corn bread (about half a 9-inch round)

1 yellow bell pepper, roasted and chopped (see Note)

2 large tomatoes, halved, seeded and chopped

1 small cucumber, chopped

1 small red onion, chopped

½ cup chopped fresh flat-leaf parsley

½ cup crumbled blue cheese

FOR THE DRESSING:

½ cup mayonnaise

¼ cup sour cream

1 tablespoon minced fresh flat-leaf parsley

½ teaspoon Homemade Beer Mustard (page 16) or coarse-grain mustard

¼ teaspoon salt

Freshly ground black pepper

1. Prepare the salad: Preheat the oven to 350°F.

2. Cut the corn bread into ¾-inch cubes. Place them in a baking pan and toast, stirring and tossing from time to time, for 20 to 30 minutes, or until the edges of the cubes are lightly browned. Remove from the oven and set aside.

3. Place the remainder of the salad ingredients in a large bowl and toss gently until combined.

4. Prepare the dressing: Combine all of the ingredients in a small bowl and mix them with a fork.

5. Just before serving, toss the salad with the corn bread. Add the dressing and toss again.

6. Transfer the salad to individual plates and serve.

Note: To roast peppers: preheat the broiler. Lightly coat whole peppers with vegetable oil and arrange them in a single layer on a baking sheet. Place in the oven and broil 5 to 6 minutes, or until the peppers are blackened in a few spots. Using tongs, turn the peppers and broil until the other side is blackened in spots. Remove from the oven and allow to cool to room temperature. Using your hands, slip off the skins, take out the core, and remove the seeds and membranes. The peppers are now ready for use.

Fried Green Tomatoes

The tomatoes you use should be bright green and as hard as a baseball.

MAKES 4 SIDE-DISH SERVINGS

4 green tomatoes

1 cup stone-ground yellow cornmeal

1 teaspoon sweet paprika

½ teaspoon freshly ground black pepper

¼ cup vegetable oil

Fried Green Tomatoes Sauce (page 75), for serving

Note: Leftover bits of green tomatoes can be chopped and combined with a little onion, some brown sugar, a splash of vinegar, a pinch of salt, and a grind or two of pepper. Heat this mixture over medium heat for about 10 minutes, or until the tomatoes are soft and the liquid is syrupy. Cool and use as a condiment for roasted meats or grilled vegetables.

1. Peel the tomatoes, cut off their ends (see Note), and cut them into ⅜-inch-thick slices.
2. Combine the cornmeal, paprika, and black pepper in a small bowl. Dip each slice in the cornmeal mixture and turn once to coat. Place the slices on a rack to dry while you dip the others.
3. Preheat the oven to 200°F.
4. Warm the oil in a 9-inch cast-iron skillet over medium heat. Add two of the slices and cook for about 3 minutes, or until the slice is golden brown on the bottom. Turn and cook for 3 minutes, or until the second side is golden brown. Remove from the skillet and place on a plate lined with paper towels to drain. Fry the remaining slices in the same manner, keeping the cooked tomatoes warm in the oven until they are all done.
5. Serve hot with Fried Green Tomatoes Sauce.

Fried Green Tomatoes Sauce

Fried green tomatoes are good, but they need a little something to go with them. A lot of people use ketchup, but you can get a lot more creative than that. Try this!

MAKES ½ CUP

½ cup Red Pepper Jelly (page 28) or store bought

2 tablespoons Creole mustard

2 teaspoons prepared horseradish

1 teaspoon coriander seeds, crushed

Combine all of the ingredients in a small bowl and refrigerate for 30 minutes before serving.

Hoppin' John Stuffed Peppers

I came up with this recipe as a way to use leftover Hoppin' John (page 60). The number of servings can be scaled up as you require (see Note).

MAKES 4 SIDE-DISH SERVINGS

2 large well-shaped bell peppers, ripe or unripe (but ripe is better)

3 cups Hoppin' John (page 60)

Sauce Piquante (page 77)

Note: For a larger number of servings, use additional peppers, more Hoppin' John, and more Sauce Piquante. The precise amounts are not important, as long as the pepper halves are nicely filled and there's plenty of sauce. To make a larger quantity, spread a layer of the Sauce Piquante in a large baking pan and place the stuffed peppers on top of it. Pour the remaining sauce over them. Cover with foil and bake in a preheated 350°F oven for 25 to 30 minutes, or until heated through.

1. Cut each pepper in half lengthwise, retaining some of the stem on each piece. Carefully remove the seeds and membranes.

2. Bring a large pot of salted water over high heat to a rolling boil. Drop in the pepper halves, reduce the heat to medium, and simmer for 1 minute. Remove from the heat. Remove the pepper halves from the pot using tongs and place them upside down on a plate lined with paper towels to drain. (The recipe can be completed up to this step in advance; if doing so, set aside now to cool to room temperature and then refrigerate.)

3. Warm the Sauce Piquante in a large, heavy-bottomed pot with a lid over low heat.

4. Stuff the pepper halves with the Hoppin' John and place them in the pot containing the sauce. Spoon the sauce over the stuffing, cover, and steam gently for 10 to 15 minutes. Remove from heat and keep covered to keep warm until ready to serve.

5. Transfer the pepper halves to individual bowls and pour the Sauce Piquante over them. Serve warm.

Sauce Piquante

Also known as "Creole sauce," this recipe has numerous variations. It can be served over just about any protein placed atop a mound of rice. I like using it in the Hoppin' John Stuffed Peppers recipe (see facing page).

MAKES APPROXIMATELY 1½ CUPS

1 tablespoon unsalted butter

½ cup chopped onion

½ cup chopped celery

½ cup chopped green bell pepper

2 garlic cloves, sliced

1 cup canned diced tomatoes with their juices

½ cup water

¼ teaspoon Worcestershire sauce

¼ teaspoon Homemade Hot Sauce (page 15) or your favorite hot sauce

¼ teaspoon salt

Freshly ground black pepper

1. Melt the butter in a heavy-bottomed pot with a lid over medium heat. Add the onion, celery, and bell pepper and cook, covered, for 2 minutes.

2. Uncover, stir, and continue cooking until the onion is translucent. Add the garlic, stir, and cook for 1 minute.

3. Add all of the remaining ingredients, stir well, and reduce the heat to medium-low. Simmer gently for 5 minutes and then remove from the heat.

4. Serve hot.

Smoky Mac and Cheese

Thomas Jefferson introduced pasta to America, and it is likely that it headed south with the numerous settlers from Virginia who crossed the mountains in the early nineteenth century. Macaroni and cheese may not be original to the mountains, but it's certainly been adopted here—now appearing on every meat-and-two menu in the region. The better the cheese is, the better the finished dish will be. If you prefer, substitute smoked Gouda for the smoked Cheddar. Mac and cheese reheats well; store leftovers in the refrigerator and bring to room temperature before reheating. Cover with foil and place in the oven at 300°F until warmed through.

MAKES 4 SIDE-DISH SERVINGS

2 tablespoons unsalted butter

1 large shallot, finely diced

Salt

2 tablespoons all-purpose flour

1 teaspoon Homemade Beer Mustard (page 16), Creole mustard, or Dijon mustard

2 cups whole milk

1 large fresh thyme sprig

6 ounces sharp Cheddar, freshly grated

2 ounces smoked Cheddar, freshly grated

1 teaspoon smoked Spanish paprika

¼ teaspoon Worcestershire sauce

¼ teaspoon Homemade Hot Sauce (page 15) or your favorite hot sauce

Freshly ground black pepper

Cooking spray

1½ cups elbow macaroni

1 tablespoon olive oil

1 cup panko bread crumbs

¼ cup freshly grated Parmesan

½ teaspoon smoked salt

½ teaspoon chopped fresh thyme leaves

1. Melt the butter in a medium saucepan over medium heat. Add the shallot and a pinch of the salt and cook, stirring occasionally, for 5 minutes. Add the flour and cook, stirring constantly, for 2 minutes, or until it browns slightly. Stir in the mustard.

2. While stirring constantly, add the milk. Cook, continuing to stir constantly, for 2 to 3 minutes, or until the sauce is smooth and bubbling. Add the thyme.

3. Reduce the heat to low and simmer for 10 minutes. Remove and discard the thyme sprig and stir in half of each of the Cheddar cheeses. Continue cooking and stirring constantly until the cheese has melted and then stir in the Worcestershire and hot sauces. Season to taste with the salt and black pepper, and reduce the heat to low to keep warm.

4. Preheat the oven to 400°F. Spray a 1½-quart baking dish with cooking spray and set aside.

5. Bring a large pot of water over high heat to a rolling boil. Add the macaroni and 1 tablespoon of the salt to the pot, reduce the heat to medium, and cook, stirring occasionally, at a gentle boil for 10 minutes, or until the macaroni is al dente. Remove from the heat and drain into a colander.

6. Pour the oil into a large mixing bowl. While the macaroni is still hot, transfer it to the bowl and stir well until thoroughly coated. Add the remaining half of each of the Cheddar cheeses to the bowl and stir until combined.

7. Remove the saucepan containing the warm cheese sauce from the heat. Fold the sauce into the bowl containing the macaroni and cheese mixture and then transfer the mixture to the prepared baking dish.

8. Combine the panko, Parmesan cheese, thyme, and smoked salt in a small bowl and sprinkle the mixture evenly over the top of the macaroni and cheese. Bake for 30 to 45 minutes, or until lightly browned on top and bubbling at the edges. Remove from the oven and serve hot.

New South Turnip Greens

Turnip greens are more popular than collards in the mountains—most likely because the cooler weather and clay soils are more conducive to growing turnips. Turnips were a dual-purpose crop for families who depended on their garden to yield all of their fresh vegetables. You could cut the greens once or twice and still be able to harvest the sweet roots at the end of the growing season. Traditionally, turnip greens were cooked in water for a long time with some form of cured pork to add seasoning. This dish requires much less time and captures the sweet, sharp flavor of the greens. Apple cider vinegar is a traditional accompaniment to greens of all types, but feel free to try other vinegars with this dish.

MAKES 2 SIDE-DISH SERVINGS

1 teaspoon olive oil

2 large garlic cloves, minced

3 green onions, green and white parts, coarsely chopped

1 cup chopped blanched turnip greens (from 4 cups fresh greens; see Note)

½ cup chicken broth

Vinegar, for serving

1. Warm the oil in a small, heavy skillet over medium heat. Add the garlic and green onions and cook, stirring occasionally, until softened. Add the turnip greens and cook, stirring, for 1 minute. Add the chicken stock, bring to a simmer, and cook, stirring once or twice, for 10 minutes, or until the broth is reduced by half. Remove from the heat.

2. Serve immediately with the vinegar for guests to add as they prefer.

Note: Thin-leaved greens, such as turnips, spinach, and mustard, hold their color better and keep longer if they are blanched while fresh. First, wash the greens and remove any tough stems or yellowed leaves. Bring a large pot of water to a rolling boil, dump in the greens, and stir with a large spoon to make sure all of them are submerged. Cook for 1 minute and then drain the greens into a colander. Rinse well under cold running water. Allow the greens to drain thoroughly and then chop or otherwise prepare them for your recipe. Blanched greens will keep in a covered container in the refrigerator for 3 days.

Killed Lettuce Salad

Hardly a spring has passed since the 1950s that I have not eaten this salad in celebration of the first vegetables of the season. My mother and grandmother made it with bacon, but at the request of a friend, I came up with this vegan variation. In this recipe, sun-dried tomatoes and soy sauce replace the salty umami of the bacon. The peas, which are also in season in early spring, add a sweet counterpoint to the bite of the vinegar. Don't try to make this with iceberg or romaine lettuce—instead, look for a pale green, loose-leaf lettuce. If you can't find fresh peas, omit them.

MAKES 4 SIDE-DISH SERVINGS

8 oil-packed sun-dried tomatoes with 2 tablespoons of the oil

6 scallions, trimmed

8 cups torn loose-leaf lettuce

10 ounces shelled fresh green peas

2 tablespoons extra virgin olive oil

2 tablespoons apple cider vinegar

1 teaspoon soy sauce

1. Slice the sun-dried tomatoes into thin shreds. Cut the scallions on the diagonal into ½-inch pieces.

2. Warm the oil from the sun-dried tomatoes and the extra virgin olive oil in a large skillet or wok over medium-high heat. Once the oil ripples, add the sun-dried tomatoes, scallions, lettuce, and peas and stir fry, for 2 minutes, or until the lettuce is wilted. Remove from the heat and stir in the vinegar and soy sauce.

3. Serve immediately.

Summer Vegetable Casserole

Cooks in the mountain South have found many creative ways to use cornmeal. Here's another one. Packed with nutritious seasonal vegetables, this dish makes a complete supper when paired with a green salad. The right time to cook this recipe is when fresh corn is abundant in your local farmers' market, and all the other vegetables should be available then, as well.

MAKES 4 TO 6 SIDE-DISH SERVINGS

1½ cups corn kernels, fresh or frozen and thawed

1 medium tomato, peeled, seeded, and chopped (see Note)

½ cup chopped red onion

½ cup chopped summer squash, any variety

½ cup chopped bell pepper, any color

1 tablespoon minced fresh flat-leaf parsley

1 teaspoon minced fresh basil

⅓ cup stone-ground cornmeal

½ teaspoon salt

¼ teaspoon freshly ground black pepper

2 large eggs

¾ cup whole milk

2 cups freshly grated Cheddar

1. Preheat the oven to 325°F. Grease a shallow, 2-quart baking dish.

2. Combine the corn kernels, tomato, onion, squash, bell pepper, parsley, basil, cornmeal, salt, and black pepper in a large mixing bowl and mix until well combined. Set the bowl aside for 30 minutes to allow the cornmeal to absorb the vegetables' juices.

3. Beat the eggs in a medium mixing bowl until the whites and yolks are thoroughly blended.

4. When the vegetable mixture is ready, transfer it to the prepared baking dish and pour the egg mixture over the top. Sprinkle with the cheese, distributing it evenly. Bake for 35 to 40 minutes, or until set and browned in a few spots on top. Remove from the oven.

5. Serve immediately.

Note: To peel and seed tomatoes, bring a large pot of water to a rolling boil. Cut an "X" on the blossom end of each tomato, just cutting through the skin, and drop the tomatoes into the boiling water. After 30 seconds, remove the tomatoes with a slotted spoon and drop them into a bowl of cold water. The skins should slip right off. To seed them, cut each tomato across its equator. Holding a tomato half over a bowl, squeeze gently to press the seeds out into the bowl. Remove the core from the stem end and chop the tomato for the recipe. Repeat with the remaining tomatoes.

Cucumber, Onion, and Tomato Salad

These summer vegetables need little more than their own juices to flavor this salad. You can substitute sweet onion, red onion, or shallots for the scallions.

MAKES 4 FIRST-COURSE SERVINGS

6 scallions, trimmed and chopped

2 small cucumbers, diced

2 medium tomatoes, cored and cut into bite-size pieces

2 teaspoons chopped fresh dill

1 teaspoon smoked salt

2 teaspoons apple cider vinegar

2 teaspoons toasted sesame oil

Freshly ground black pepper

1. Combine the scallions, cucumber, tomato, dill, and smoked salt in a bowl and set aside at room temperature for 15 minutes.

2. Add the vinegar and sesame oil, along with a few grinds of the black pepper, and toss.

3. Transfer to serving plates and serve immediately.

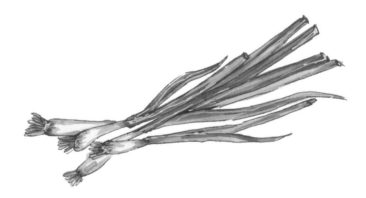

Southern Vegetable Stir Fry

The flavors of the mountains are captured here in an easy stir fry that would make a great week-night dinner. Turnips are the most popular greens in the mountains, but you can use collards, mustard, kale, or a combination. Thicker-leaved greens may require a longer cooking time. You could substitute navy beans, lady peas, White Acre peas, or crowder peas for the black-eyed peas.

MAKES 4 MAIN-DISH SERVINGS

3 bacon slices, chopped

2 tablespoons vegetable oil

1½ cups chopped onion

1 cup chopped celery

1 cup chopped green bell pepper

1 teaspoon salt

¼ teaspoon freshly ground black pepper

2 garlic cloves, minced

1 bay leaf

3 cups chopped and stemmed greens

One 15-ounce can black-eyed peas, drained and rinsed

1. Cook the bacon in a large saucepan over medium-high heat until browned. Remove from the heat and, using a slotted spoon, transfer the bacon pieces to a plate lined with paper towels. Set aside.

2. Pour off all but 1 tablespoon of the bacon drippings in the saucepan. Add the oil to the saucepan and return it to medium heat. Add the onion, celery, bell pepper, salt, and black pepper and cook, stirring occasionally, until the onion is translucent. Add the garlic and bay leaf and cook for 2 minutes, or until the garlic is pale golden.

3. Add the greens and cook for about 5 minutes, or until they are barely tender. Stir in the black-eyed peas and the cooked bacon and remove from the heat. Remove and discard the bay leaf, taste for seasoning, and adjust as needed.

4. Serve hot.

Country-Style Cobb Salad

Cobb salad was invented by Bob Cobb, a restaurant owner in Hollywood, in 1937, and it has become an iconic American dish. This version uses ingredients that are popular on both sides of the mountains, while remaining true to the spirit of the original.

MAKES 2 MAIN-DISH SERVINGS

FOR THE DRESSING:

4 teaspoons apple cider vinegar

½ teaspoon salt

¼ teaspoon coarsely ground black pepper

¼ teaspoon Worcestershire sauce

¼ teaspoon Dijon mustard

Pinch of sugar

⅓ cup extra virgin olive oil

FOR THE SALAD:

3 cups torn lettuce or other tender greens

Handful fresh nasturtium leaves (optional; see Note)

1 medium tomato, chopped

8 to 10 cucumber slices

6 yellow cherry tomatoes, halved

6 radishes, trimmed and halved

2 green onions, trimmed and chopped

1 Pickled Egg (page 12) or hard-boiled egg, halved (see page 176)

2 tablespoons crumbled blue cheese

2 bacon strips, cooked and crumbled

Nasturtium blossoms, for garnish (optional)

1. Chill 2 serving plates for 1 hour prior to serving the salad.

2. Prepare the dressing: Combine all of the dressing ingredients in a small bowl and whisk with a fork to emulsify. Set aside.

3. Prepare the salad: Arrange equal portions of the lettuce on each of the chilled plates. Arrange the remaining ingredients on top of the lettuce beds. Whisk the dressing again and drizzle it over the salad.

4. Serve immediately.

Note: You can easily grow nasturtiums from seed in a window box or planter. They also sometimes show up at farmers' markets. Substitute mustard greens or arugula if nasturtiums are unavailable.

SEQUATCHIE COVE CREAMERY

Sequatchie Cove is a geological anomaly that lies at the westernmost edge of East Tennessee, in the shadow of the Cumberland Plateau. The valley, cut by the Sequatchie River, runs northeast to southwest in a line so near to straight that it can be seen clearly in satellite images. There, in one of the nooks known as Coppinger Cove, lies the 300-acre Sequatchie Cove Farm, its herd of dairy cattle, and the Sequatchie Cove Creamery, which began operations in 2010.

The cheeses produced here are reminiscent of those of the Savoie region of France, with outstanding blue varieties, Shakerag Blue and Bellamy Blue, among a total of seven offerings. The farm uses no pesticides, chemical fertilizers, antibiotics, or growth hormones, and runs entirely on solar power. Whey, a byproduct of cheesemaking, is fed to the farm's hogs. The folks at Sequatchie Cove Creamery are regulars at the seasonal Chattanooga Farmers' Market, and they also ship their products anywhere (see Sources, page 183).

A Plate of Three Greens

We always have an abundance of fresh greens available in late summer, and I came up with this warm salad combination to use them up. It's unlikely that you'll be able to get your hands on sweet potato greens—unless, of course, you grow them in your garden. Feel free to substitute whatever fresh greens are available.

MAKES 2 SIDE-DISH SERVINGS

FOR THE SWEET POTATO GREENS:

1 tablespoon vegetable oil

½ cup chopped onion

1 cup bite-size pieces sweet potato greens

1 teaspoon sorghum syrup

2 teaspoons balsamic vinegar

FOR THE COLLARD GREENS:

1 tablespoon olive oil

1 tablespoon minced fresh garlic

1 cup sliced collard greens (cut into ribbons)

Zest and juice of ½ lemon

FOR THE DANDELION GREENS:

1 bacon strip

¼ cup chopped (in ½-inch pieces) scallions, white and green parts

1 cup bite-size pieces dandelion greens

2 teaspoons apple cider vinegar

Coarse sea salt

Freshly ground black pepper

Hot sauce, for serving

1. Preheat the oven to 200°F. Place three heatproof bowls and two serving plates in the warm oven.

2. Prepare the sweet potato greens: Warm the vegetable oil in a heavy, cast-iron skillet over medium heat. Add the onion, reduce the heat to medium-low, and cook, stirring occasionally, until the onion is uniformly golden brown. Add the sweet potato greens and stir until they are just wilted. Remove from the heat and transfer to a heatproof bowl. Drizzle with the sorghum syrup and balsamic vinegar and toss to coat. Transfer the greens to one of the heatproof bowls and return it to the oven.

3. Prepare the collard greens: Wipe the skillet clean and add the olive oil and garlic. Cook gently over medium-low heat until the garlic is barely colored and then add the collard greens. Cook, stirring occasionally, for 3 to 5 minutes, until the greens are wilted and tender. Remove from the heat and transfer to a second heatproof bowl. Sprinkle with the lemon zest and drizzle with the lemon juice. Toss to coat. Transfer the greens to one of the heatproof bowls and return it to the oven.

4. Prepare the dandelion greens: Wipe the skillet clean again and add the bacon. Fry over medium heat until the bacon is browned. Remove the bacon to a plate lined with paper towels using a slotted spoon and set aside.

5. Add the scallions and dandelion greens to the bacon drippings remaining in the skillet and cook until the greens are wilted and tender, about 3 minutes. Remove from the heat.

Add the apple cider vinegar and stir. Transfer the greens to the remaining heatproof bowl.

6. To serve, remove the heatproof bowls and the plates from the oven. Pile equal portions of each of the greens on the warmed serving plates. Chop up the cooked bacon and sprinkle equal portions of it over each of the servings. Sprinkle each serving with the salt and black pepper.

7. Serve with the hot sauce.

Okra and Tomatoes

Make this recipe for people who say they don't like okra because of its sliminess. Browning the okra and adding acid in the form of tomatoes changes the chemistry of its juices and avoids the slime. The recipe makes a perfect side dish for any meat-and-two dinner, and the leftovers can be added to vegetable soup to create a gumbo.

MAKES 4 SIDE-DISH SERVINGS

1 pound fresh okra

1 tablespoon bacon drippings or vegetable oil

3 fresh, ripe tomatoes, cored, peeled, and coarsely chopped

3 garlic cloves, minced

1 small fresh green jalapeño pepper, stemmed and chopped

½ teaspoon salt

¼ teaspoon Highland Heat Seasoning (page 17)

¼ teaspoon Worcestershire sauce

1. Wipe the okra pods with a kitchen towel to remove any debris and slice them cross-wise into ½-inch slices; discard the stem ends.
2. Warm the bacon drippings in a heavy, cast-iron skillet over medium heat until they begin to ripple. Stir in the okra and cook for 6 minutes, or until many pieces show some browning. Add all of the remaining ingredients and stir well.
3. Reduce the heat to medium-low and simmer for 10 minutes, or until the tomatoes begin to break down. Remove from the heat.
4. Serve hot.

Old-Fashioned Coleslaw

My grandmother made this dressing frequently when cabbage was in season. The technique is based on a recipe contributed by Mrs. B. I. Hughes to the *Knoxville 1901 Cookbook*. I modified the recipe by taking into consideration the fact that heaped measures were used in 1900. If you don't like the idea of black specks in the pale-colored dressing, use white pepper instead of black.

MAKES 6 TO 8 SIDE-DISH SERVINGS

⅓ cup whole milk, at room temperature

½ teaspoon cornstarch

1 large egg, separated, at room temperature

2 tablespoons plus 2 teaspoons granulated sugar

1 tablespoon unsalted butter, melted

½ teaspoon salt

½ teaspoon mustard powder

Freshly ground black pepper

⅓ cup apple cider vinegar

1 medium head white cabbage, trimmed, cored, and finely chopped

1. Add 1 tablespoon of the milk to a small bowl and dissolve the cornstarch in it. Reserve this mixture.

2. Bring 1 inch of water to a simmer in a saucepan over medium heat.

3. In a metal bowl that will fit on top of the saucepan containing the water, stir together the egg yolk, sugar, butter, salt, mustard, and a few grinds of the black pepper until the ingredients are well combined. Stir in the remaining milk.

4. Set the metal bowl over the saucepan and stir frequently. The water in the saucepan must be bubbling; steaming is not hot enough. After you have cooked the mixture for about 3 minutes, or once steam begins to rise from the bowl, stir in the cornstarch mixture. Cook, stirring frequently, for 5 minutes, or until the mixture begins to thicken slightly.

5. Stir in the vinegar, 1 teaspoon at a time, and continue cooking, while stirring constantly, for 8 to 12 minutes, or until the mixture is smooth. Remove the bowl from the saucepan, dry off the bottom, and set aside away from the heat. Remove the saucepan from the heat.

6. In a medium mixing bowl, beat the egg white with a wire whisk until it holds soft peaks. Fold the beaten egg white into the dressing in the metal bowl. Set the dressing aside to cool to room temperature.

7. Place the chopped cabbage in a large mixing bowl and toss with the dressing. Store in the refrigerator for at least 1 hour, or until well chilled, before serving.

8. Serve.

Asparagus with Black Walnut Pesto

Gathering black walnuts in autumn provided an opportunity for a family outing. My mom, my grandfather, and I would head out to the woods with burlap sacks and fill them with walnuts and hickory nuts. Once we were back at the house, it was my job to separate the walnuts from the smaller hickory nuts, and to strew the walnuts, still in their green husks, in the gravel driveway. Once they'd been placed there, my grandfather would run over them a few times with his car. That would free the nuts, but there was still considerable effort involved with cracking and separating the kernels.

In order to have asparagus and black walnuts at the same time, you'll need to use stored walnuts from the previous season or asparagus forced for autumn production. Walnut kernels can be frozen for 6 months, but I prefer to purchase imported asparagus and make this when the walnuts are freshly shelled.

MAKES 2 SIDE-DISH SERVINGS

12 to 16 fresh asparagus spears

Pinch of sugar

½ cup chopped black walnuts

1 cup packed fresh spinach leaves

4 tablespoons (½ stick) unsalted butter

¼ cup freshly grated Parmigiano-Reggiano

¼ cup chopped fresh flat-leaf parsley

2 teaspoons chopped fresh tarragon

1 teaspoon apple cider vinegar

4 to 6 tablespoons extra virgin olive oil

Salt

1. Snap off the lower portion of the asparagus spears. Fill a tall glass halfway full of cold water and add the sugar. Place the tops of the asparagus in the glass and set aside at room temperature for 1 hour. (This step is not necessary if the asparagus is very fresh.)

2. Place the walnuts in a small, heavy skillet over medium heat. Cook, stirring and tossing frequently, until the walnuts begin to brown and become fragrant. Remove from the heat and set aside to cool.

3. Bring a medium saucepan of salted water to a rolling boil. Drop in the spinach, making sure it is fully submerged by pressing down with a spoon. Return to a boil, remove from the heat, and immediately drain the spinach into a colander.

4. Refresh the spinach under cold running water and then drain it thoroughly, squeezing out any excess liquid with your hands.

5. Transfer the spinach to the bowl of a food processor. Add the toasted walnuts, butter, cheese, parsley, tarragon, and vinegar and pulse until a coarse paste forms. Add the oil, 1 tablespoon at a time, and pulse until the pesto reaches a pleasing consistency (you may not need all of the oil). Season with salt to taste. If you don't own a food processor, you can make the pesto in the traditional way, using a mortar and pestle.

6. Transfer the pesto to a bowl and cover it with plastic wrap, pressing down on the wrap so it adheres to the surface of the pesto (this will prevent darkening). Refrigerate if not using right away; bring to room temperature before serving.

7. Preheat the oven to 200°F. Place 2 serving plates in the warm oven.

8. Bring a large pot of water to a boil and drop in the asparagus. Once the water returns to a boil, cook for 3 minutes. Remove from the heat, drain into a colander, and immediately transfer the asparagus to the warmed plates. Add a dollop of the pesto to each plate.

9. Serve with the remaining pesto.

Fried Taters and Onions

Fried taters were standard fare for both breakfast and dinner at my grandmother's house, and they were invariably seasoned with onions. Parboiling the potatoes helps keep them from becoming greasy in the skillet. You can endlessly vary this recipe by adding other diced vegetables, such as bell peppers or summer squash, which produces a colorful vegetable hash that makes a great side for any protein, from beans to fish.

MAKES 2 SIDE-DISH SERVINGS

3 medium potatoes

Salt

2 tablespoons bacon drippings

1 small onion, diced

Freshly ground black pepper

1. Place the potatoes, unpeeled, in a large pot. Add enough water to cover them by 1 inch and set the pot over high heat. Add 1 teaspoon of salt and bring to a boil. Reduce the heat to medium to keep the potatoes at a steady simmer and cook, uncovered, for 15 minutes, or until a wooden skewer pierces the largest potato with little resistance. Drain the potatoes into a colander and set aside.

2. When the potatoes are cool enough to handle, peel them and cut into ½-inch dice. You should have approximately 4 cups of diced potatoes.

3. Warm the bacon drippings in a 12-inch cast-iron skillet until they are fragrant and add the diced potatoes. Cook, undisturbed, until the bottom layer is lightly browned, 4 to 5 minutes. Turn the potatoes with a spatula, add the diced onion, and continue to cook, tossing now and then, for 6 to 7 minutes, or until many of the potatoes are browned and the onion is translucent. Season with salt and black pepper to taste.

4. Serve warm; if you are not serving immediately, keep the potatoes warm in a 200°F oven until you are ready to serve.

New Potato Salad

When potato vines have blooms, you can dig down with your fingers around the base of the plant and steal a few "new" potatoes. Look for new potatoes in farmers' markets around the summer solstice in the mountain South. Ideally, you should be able to rub the skin off with your fingers. As a second choice, use the tiny, uniform potatoes offered at some supermarkets. This potato salad is best when allowed to sit overnight in the refrigerator, permitting the flavors to meld.

MAKES 4 TO 6 SIDE-DISH SERVINGS

3 pounds new potatoes

¼ cup Homemade Beer Mustard (page 16) or other good coarse-grain mustard

1½ teaspoons apple cider vinegar

1½ teaspoons granulated sugar

4 large eggs, hard-boiled and peeled (see page 176)

6 green onions, white and green parts, chopped

2 celery stalks, finely diced

½ cup chopped Sweet Lime Cucumber Pickles (page 3) or your favorite sweet pickles

Salt

Freshly ground black pepper

½ cup (approximately) mayonnaise

Minced fresh flat-leaf parsley, for garnish

Paprika, for garnish

1. Wash the potatoes, but do not peel them.
2. Bring a large pot of water over high heat to a boil. Add the potatoes, reduce the heat to medium, and cook them until the point of a knife meets little resistance when you pierce a potato; start checking after 15 minutes, but the exact time will depend upon the size of the potatoes, the amount of water, and so forth. Remove from the heat. Drain the potatoes and rinse them briefly under cold running water. Set aside to cool slightly.
3. While the potatoes are cooking, stir together the mustard, vinegar, and sugar in a large mixing bowl until the sugar dissolves.
4. Once the potatoes have cooled, cut them into bite-size pieces. Add them to the bowl containing the mustard mixture and toss well. Allow to cool to room temperature before you proceed.
5. Chop the eggs and add them to the bowl containing the potatoes. Add the onion, celery, and Sweet Lime Cucumber Pickles and stir until well combined. Season with salt and black pepper to taste.
6. Stir in the mayonnaise, a little at a time, until the salad holds together and is as moist as you like. Cover and refrigerate for at least 2 hours before serving.
7. Garnish with the parsley and paprika and serve.

Mushroom and Potato Soup

My mother made potato soup often, and she never bothered with a recipe. Onions, celery, potatoes, water, and milk were the main ingredients, and it made for a simple and, when accompanied by a wedge of hot, buttered corn bread, sufficient weeknight dinner. I've taken her basic idea and added mushrooms—the earthiness goes well with the potatoes—and a few roasted peppers for a touch of sweetness and vibrant color. Broth and heavy whipping cream make this a rich and elegant dish that's suitable as a first course for a special dinner.

MAKES 4 FIRST-COURSE SERVINGS

2 tablespoons unsalted butter

½ small onion, chopped

1 celery rib, chopped

8 ounces mushrooms, coarsely chopped (see Note)

¼ teaspoon kosher salt

2 cups chicken broth

1 pound potatoes, peeled and cut into bite-size pieces (about 3 medium potatoes) (see Note)

1 fresh rosemary sprig

1 bay leaf

½ cup heavy whipping cream

Freshly grated nutmeg

Freshly ground white pepper

2 tablespoons minced roasted sweet pepper, any color

1. Preheat the oven to 200°F. Place 4 serving bowls in the warm oven.

2. Warm the butter in a large saucepan or Dutch oven over medium-low heat. Add the onion and celery, cover, and cook gently until the vegetables are softened. Stir in the mushrooms and salt and cook, uncovered and stirring occasionally, for 5 to 7 minutes,

or until the mushrooms have darkened and released their juices.

3.   Add the broth, the potatoes, the rosemary, and the bay leaf. Reduce the heat to medium-low to maintain a simmer, partially cover, and cook for 20 to 25 minutes, or until the potatoes are tender.

4.   Stir in the cream and continue cooking until the liquid returns to a simmer. Remove from the heat, cover, and set aside in a warm place to steep for 10 minutes.

5.   Remove and discard the rosemary and bay leaf. Add a grating or two of the nutmeg and a few grinds of the white pepper. Taste for seasoning and adjust as needed.

6.   Ladle the soup into the warmed bowls. Garnish with the roasted sweet pepper and serve immediately.

Notes: You can make this soup with white-button or other cultivated mushrooms, but for a truly memorable dish, use locally foraged chanterelles. These yellow-orange beauties have a hint of apricot aroma and flavor. Of course, other wild mushrooms can also be used.

I like this dish best when it is made with Yukon Gold potatoes. Regionally popular potato varieties include Irish Cobbler, Kennebec, and Red Pontiac; any potato suitable for potato salad will give good results in this recipe.

Sweet Potato Casserole

A potluck and church supper favorite for many years, this easy casserole can be made with fresh or canned sweet potatoes. I find that roasting the potatoes produces a better texture than boiling them, but boiling is fine, too. Hickory nuts appear at farmers' markets in autumn. If you can't find them, look for native, nonhybrid pecans or use regular pecans or walnuts instead.

MAKES 4 TO 6 SIDE-DISH SERVINGS

FOR THE CASSEROLE:

3 medium sweet potatoes

½ cup granulated sugar

1 large egg

½ teaspoon vanilla extract

3 tablespoons whole milk

4 tablespoons (½ stick) unsalted butter, melted

FOR THE TOPPING:

¼ cup light brown sugar

¼ cup all-purpose flour

¼ cup chopped hickory nuts

1 tablespoon plus 1 teaspoon unsalted butter, melted

1. Prepare the casserole: Position a rack in the top third of the oven and preheat to 375°F.

2. Scrub the sweet potatoes, pierce each potato with a fork, and place them directly on the oven rack. Bake for 30 minutes, or until the potatoes are tender. Remove from the oven and set aside to cool to room temperature.

3. Remove and discard the sweet potatoes' skins, which should slip off easily, and place the flesh in a mixing bowl. (The sweet potatoes can be prepared up to this point several days in advance; if doing so, store them, covered, in the refrigerator and bring to room temperature before proceeding with the recipe.)

4. Reheat the oven to 350°F.

5. Mash the sweet potatoes with the sugar until well combined.

6. Beat together the egg, milk, and vanilla in a separate mixing bowl. Stir this mixture into the sweet potatoes until well combined, and then add the butter. Transfer the mixture to a casserole dish.

7. Prepare the topping: Combine the brown sugar, flour, and nuts in a small bowl. Stir in the butter until well combined.

8. Distribute the topping evenly over the surface of the casserole. Bake for 25 minutes. Remove from the oven if serving immediately; if not, reduce the oven temperature to 200°F and keep warm until ready to serve.

9. Serve warm.

Chapter Four

FIELD, FOREST, AND STREAM

Hogs arrived in the American south along with the Spanish, who were in the habit of turning them loose to fatten on whatever food was available. Feral hogs remain a problem in the mountains nearly 500 years later.

Cultivated hogs, on the other hand, remain a source of regional pride, as skilled artisans turn them into country ham and bacon with an international reputation for quality. Cattle graze on lush pasture in the river bottoms, yielding fine, lean beef with excellent flavor. Chickens have always been a fixture of the rural farmstead, and these days, most cities in the region allow people to keep backyard chickens.

Before our pristine streams were rendered unsafe by various forms of pollution, even the poorest folk had access to a source of protein if they could catch a few crawdads and maybe land a catfish. These days, the catfish, trout, and even the crawdads come from aquaculture more often than not.

Although we have dozens of vegetable dishes, Southern Appalachian folks love their animal protein.

Meatloaf with Wild Mushrooms

Many kinds of edible wild mushrooms grow in the forests of East Tennessee and western North Carolina. Foraged mushrooms turn up at farmers' markets from summer through fall. I wrote this recipe with dried mushrooms, which are widely available in well-stocked grocery stores, in mind. Porcini mushrooms are a good choice. Any fresh wild mushrooms are even better in this recipe, so use whatever is available. For authentic mountain beef flavor, choose local, grass-fed beef. I sometimes serve this with my Sauce Piquante (page 77) instead of the rich mushroom gravy.

MAKES 4 TO 6 MAIN-DISH SERVINGS

FOR THE MEATLOAF:

½ ounce dried wild mushrooms (see Notes)

1¾ cups hot water

¼ cup old-fashioned oatmeal (not quick-cooking)

1 teaspoon sea salt

¼ teaspoon freshly ground black pepper

¼ teaspoon celery seeds

2 tablespoons unsalted butter

¼ cup minced green bell pepper

1 shallot, minced

1 garlic clove, minced

1 pound ground chuck

½ teaspoon dried thyme

FOR THE GRAVY:

1 tablespoon bacon drippings

1 small shallot, minced

2 tablespoons chopped mushrooms

1 tablespoon all-purpose flour

1 cup mushroom soaking water (see Notes)

¼ teaspoon Worcestershire sauce

Salt

Freshly ground black pepper

Minced fresh flat-leaf parsley, for garnish

1.   Prepare the meatloaf: Place the dried mushrooms in a small metal bowl and cover with the hot water. (The water should be hot enough to make tea, but not boiling.) Set aside to soak for 30 minutes.

2.   Drain the mushrooms and reserve the water. Trim off and discard any woody portions and chop the mushrooms. (If using fresh mushrooms, wipe, trim, and chop them, then proceed as below.) Set aside a third of the mushrooms to make the gravy.

3.   Preheat the oven to 350°F. Line a 9-by-12-inch baking pan with heavy-duty aluminum foil.

4.   Combine the oatmeal and ¼ cup of the reserved mushroom soaking water in a large mixing bowl. Add the salt, black pepper, and celery seeds.

10. Remove the meatloaf from the oven and set aside for at least 10 minutes to rest.

11. Slice the meatloaf and serve with the mushroom gravy ladled over it; garnish with the parsley.

5. Melt the butter in a small skillet over medium heat. Add the mushrooms, bell pepper, shallot, and garlic and sauté until the shallot is translucent. Remove from the heat.

6. Scrape the contents of the skillet into the bowl containing the other ingredients and mix well. Add the beef and thyme and mix gently with your hands until the mixture is well combined.

7. Shape the mixture into a small loaf, place in the prepared pan, and bake for 45 minutes to 1 hour, or until an instant-read thermometer inserted in the thickest part of the loaf registers 165°F. Remove from the oven.

8. Prepare the gravy: Warm the bacon drippings in a medium saucepan over medium heat. Add the shallot and mushrooms and cook, stirring often, until the shallot is translucent. Add the flour and stir until well combined. Cook, stirring often, for 1 minute.

9. Stir in the remaining reserved mushroom soaking water and cook, stirring constantly, until the gravy is thickened and smooth. Remove from the heat and stir in the Worcestershire sauce. Taste for seasoning and season with the salt and black pepper to taste. If not using immediately, return to low heat to keep the sauce warm until you are ready to serve.

Notes: After soaking the mushrooms, be sure to strain out and discard any sediment that accumulates in the soaking water before you reserve it. You should have 1¼ cups of soaking water; if not, use beef stock or water to make up the difference.

If using fresh mushrooms, substitute beef stock for the soaking water.

Ultimate Meatloaf Sandwich

Meatloaf is a standard entrée on the menu of dozens of meat-and-two restaurants, an East Tennessee tradition. Unlike Meatloaf with Wild Mushrooms (page 102), this recipe will hold its shape well when cold, making it ideal for slicing. Slices of meatloaf can be made into great sandwiches with mustard, mayonnaise, and radishes. If you haven't the time to make Homemade Beer Mustard, substitute any good coarse-grained mustard.

MAKES 4 TO 5 SANDWICHES

FOR THE MEATLOAF:

1 pound ground chuck

1 cup chopped onions

⅔ cup quick-cooking oats or old-fashioned oats chopped in a food processor

½ cup ketchup

½ cup chopped fresh flat-leaf parsley

2 large eggs, well beaten

¾ teaspoon dried thyme

½ teaspoon salt

¼ teaspoon freshly ground black pepper

FOR THE SANDWICHES:

Radishes

Salt

8 to 10 whole-grain sandwich bread slices

Homemade Beer Mustard (page 16) or coarse-grain mustard

Mayonnaise

Alfalfa sprouts, for garnish

1. Prepare the meatloaf: Preheat the oven to 350°F.

2. Combine all of the ingredients in a large mixing bowl and mix well with your hands; take care to not overmix. (Wetting your hands first will help keep the mixture from sticking to them.)

3. Spoon the mixture into a standard-size loaf pan. Smooth down the top, but take care not to pack the mixture too tightly—the resulting loaf will be too dense. Bake for 1 hour. Remove from the oven and set aside to cool slightly.

4. Carefully pour off any liquid that has accumulated in the pan and then tip the loaf on to a serving plate for slicing. Set aside to cool for 15 minutes before attempting to slice (better yet, refrigerate it overnight).

5. Prepare the sandwiches: Wash and trim the radishes and slice them into very thin slices. Place the slices in a bowl and sprinkle with a big pinch of the salt. Set aside for 15 minutes.

6. For each sandwich, spread the Home-made Beer Mustard on 1 slice of bread and spread mayonnaise on the other.

7. Slice the meatloaf into ½-inch-thick slices. Place 1 slice on top of each of the bread slices coated with the mustard. Arrange a few of the radish slices on top of the meatloaf slice and garnish with alfalfa sprouts. Top with the mayonnaise-coated bread slices.

8. Serve.

MEAT-AND-TWO

In the introduction, I mentioned the long tradition of innkeeping in the mountains of North Carolina and Tennessee. One of the keys to building a reputation as a worthy innkeeper was providing an abundant table that was necessarily spread with seasonal delicacies and standards from the smokehouse and cellar.

This tradition lives on today in restaurants that specialize in "meat-and-two" menus. Typically, they offer a daily selection of meats and six, ten, or more side dishes, and guests can choose one meat and two sides for a set price. Biscuits, corn muffins, corn griddle cakes, or rolls also usually come with the plate, and sometimes, a drink and dessert are included, too.

You can bring the concept home by putting on your very own buffet for a crowd. Make Meatloaf with Wild Mushrooms (page 102) and Skillet-Fried Chicken with Gravy (page 124) and set them out with a selection of side dishes chosen from the recipes in Chapters One, Two, and Three.

Skillet Beef and Mac

Here's my take on an old comfort-food favorite from church suppers and family reunions. My mom never wrote down a recipe for this dish, and thus, it was a little different every time she made it. My version aims toward hers, but has some additional kicks.

MAKES 4 TO 6 MAIN-DISH SERVINGS

1 tablespoon vegetable oil

1 pound ground chuck

1 medium onion, chopped

1 small green bell pepper, stemmed, seeded, and chopped

1 celery rib, chopped

1 garlic clove, minced

1 teaspoon Creole Three Seasoning (page 18)

½ teaspoon Highland Heat Seasoning (page 17)

½ teaspoon salt

¼ teaspoon dried thyme leaves

One 8-ounce can tomato sauce

1 cup water

1 tablespoon salt

1 cup elbow macaroni

Salt

Freshly ground black pepper

1 cup grated smoked Gouda or Cheddar

1. Warm the oil in a large, cast-iron skillet over medium heat. Add the ground chuck and cook, stirring occasionally, for 15 minutes. Using a slotted spoon, transfer the meat to a bowl and set aside. Pour off and discard all but 1 tablespoon of the fat remaining in the skillet.

2. Return the skillet to medium heat, add the onion, and cook for 3 minutes. Add the green pepper and celery and cook for 3 minutes. Add the garlic, Creole Three Seasoning, Highland Heat Seasoning, salt, and thyme and cook for 1 minute.

3. Reduce the heat to medium-low and add the reserved beef, tomato sauce, and water and to the skillet. Simmer for 10 minutes.

4. Preheat the broiler.

5. Bring a large pot of water to a boil and add the macaroni. Cook at a slow boil for 8 minutes. Remove from the heat. Drain the macaroni into a colander and add it to the skillet. Simmer for 1 minute. Taste for seasoning and season with the salt and black pepper to taste. Remove from the heat.

6. Sprinkle the cheese over the ingredients in the skillet and place the skillet under the broiler for 3 minutes, or until the cheese is melted and beginning to brown in spots.

7. Serve the casserole directly from the skillet.

Country-Style Beef Stew

I've based this Country-Style Beef Stew on my mother's recipe, which was a reliable winter-time warmer at our house. Mother worked for more than 50 years as the bookkeeper for the Farmers Livestock Market in Greeneville, Tennessee. We sometimes received a gift of fresh beef from one of her many acquaintances in the industry. The key to this recipe is to brown the beef slowly, adding only as much fat as necessary to produce a crisp outer crust. Don't salt the beef before cooking, as salting will cause it to release moisture, which inhibits browning. Serve the stew with corn bread or hot biscuits.

MAKES 4 TO 6 MAIN-DISH SERVINGS

½ cup all-purpose flour

½ teaspoon freshly ground black pepper

1 to 1¼ pounds chuck roast, cut into 1-inch cubes

1 to 2 tablespoons bacon drippings

1 medium onion, chopped

1 celery rib with leaves, chopped

1 garlic clove, minced

2 bay leaves

1 teaspoon finely chopped fresh flat-leaf parsley stems

½ teaspoon dried thyme

⅛ teaspoon celery seeds

2 cups beef stock

Salt

3 medium potatoes, peeled and cut into 1-inch pieces

2 large carrots, peeled and cut into 1-inch pieces

Chopped fresh flat-leaf parsley leaves, for garnish

1. Stir together the flour and black pepper in a large mixing bowl. Add the cubed chuck roast and toss to coat each cube thoroughly.

2. Warm 1 tablespoon of the bacon drippings in a large saucepan or Dutch oven over medium heat until they begin to ripple. Working in batches, add the chuck roast cubes—taking care not to crowd the pan—and cook, turning the pieces

with tongs, until they are browned on all sides. Remove the brown pieces to a heat-proof bowl and continue until all the beef is browned, adding additional bacon drippings, 1 teaspoon at a time, as needed to prevent the beef from sticking. The process will take between 30 and 45 minutes.

3. When all of the cubes are browned, add the onion to the saucepan and sauté for 5 minutes. Add the celery, garlic, bay leaves, parsley stems, thyme, and celery seeds and cook, stirring once or twice, for 5 minutes.

4. Raise the heat to medium-high and add the beef stock. Bring to a boil, stirring and scraping up any browned bits from the bottom of the pot. When the stew is smooth and bubbling, add the cooked chuck roast cubes and any of their accumulated juices.

5. Reduce the heat to medium-low to maintain a slow simmer, cover, and cook gently for 1½ hours, or until the beef is tender enough to cut with the side of a spoon.

6. While the stew simmers, bring a large pot of salted water over high heat to a boil. Add the potatoes and carrots, reduce the heat to medium, and simmer for 15 minutes. Remove from the heat.

7. Drain the potatoes and carrots into a colander and add them to the stew for the last 30 minutes of cooking. Taste for seasoning and add salt and black pepper as needed. Remove from the heat.

8. Ladle the stew into serving bowls and serve garnished with the parsley leaves.

Country Ham with Redeye Gravy

Salt-cured country ham has been a staple in the Appalachian region since the earliest settlers arrived here. The curing method is similar to that used to produce the famous Iberico hams of Spain. Allan Benton, whose pork products have brought worldwide acclaim to his small business in Madisonville, Tennessee, sells both "young" hams, which have been hanging for about a year, and fine, longer-aged hams that rival the best prosciutto. As the story goes, redeye gravy was invented at one of the many inns that once dotted the East Tennessee landscape, by a cook who liked to drink. Supposedly, Andrew Jackson came in one day and ordered ham with his breakfast—and requested "some of that gravy as red as your eyes" to be served with it. Serve this dish with biscuits, such as Easy Buttermilk Biscuits (page 172). If your ham is already cut into large slices, cut the slices into 4-inch squares for this recipe.

MAKES 2 MAIN-DISH SERVINGS

2 teaspoons bacon drippings

3 ounces country ham slices

1 cup strong black coffee

2 teaspoons light brown sugar

Easy Buttermilk Biscuits (page 172), for serving

1. Warm the bacon drippings in a cast-iron skillet over medium heat. Add the ham slices, taking care not to crowd the pan, and cook for 3 minutes on each side, or until the fat on the ham is translucent and the lean portion has darkened in color (do not brown the slices, or they will become tough). Remove the warmed ham slices from the skillet and set aside, covered, to keep warm.

2. As soon as all of the ham has been warmed, pour the coffee into the skillet and add the brown sugar. Reduce the heat to medium-low and simmer gently for 1 minute. Keep warm until ready to serve.

3. Open a biscuit and place it on a plate. Place a slice of ham on each biscuit half. Ladle the redeye gravy over the biscuits and ham.

BENTON'S SMOKY MOUNTAIN COUNTRY HAMS

Prior to my first meeting with Allan Benton at his place of business in Madisonville, Tennessee, he'd always seemed larger than life. Benton's Smoky Mountain Country Hams products have been lauded by celebrity chefs from David Chang to Sean Brock to just about everybody else who uses bacon in their kitchens.

"Please, call me Allan," he said, when I tried to address him as "Mr. Benton." He modestly insisted that his secrets amounted to nothing more than maintaining a tradition born centuries ago. Benton makes his products only from heritage-breed hogs, smokes them "just enough," and hangs them up to age properly before sale. This process requires not only skill, but patience. His best hams are aged for more than 12 months, and they continue to improve with another year of aging. Select older hams are thinly sliced and offered as "Tennessee prosciutto." As I talked with Benton about his company, I could see the hams hanging from rustic wooden racks.

"Come back soon," he said, as my husband, Jerry, and I prepared to leave with our selections all neatly vacuum-sealed in plastic. Our reception at Benton's Smoky Mountain Country Hams was so warm that we felt as though we'd made a new friend.

Slow-Cooker Pork Shoulder

You don't need a smoker and a pile of hickory wood in order to enjoy the flavors of Southern barbecue—you can make delicious pulled pork in a slow cooker. The Spanish paprika used in this recipe adds a hint of smoke, as if the meat had been kissed by hickory. Tell your guests how you did it, if you want to, but most will assume the dish is authentic barbecue. I prefer not to salt the meat before cooking, as salt tends to draw out the juices, resulting in a less succulent product. Add salt at the end of cooking, if you wish, or leave it to your guests to season to their taste. Try the pork with any of the barbecue sauces found on page 20.

MAKES 4 TO 6 MAIN-DISH SERVINGS

One 2- to 3-pound boneless Boston butt pork roast

¼ teaspoon freshly ground black pepper

¼ teaspoon smoked Spanish paprika

¼ teaspoon Highland Heat Seasoning (page 17)

1 small onion, chopped

½ cup water

1. Bring the pork to room temperature prior to cooking.

2. Combine the seasonings in a small bowl. Scatter the onion in the bottom of the slow cooker. Distribute the seasoning mix evenly over the pork and place the pork and the water in the slow cooker.

3. Set the cooker on "low" and cook for about 7 hours, or until the pork is tender when pierced with a fork.

4. Remove the pork from the cooker and set it aside on a tray to cool slightly.

5. When the pork is cool enough to handle, shred it with your fingers or two forks. Keep it warm in a 200°F oven until ready to serve or cool completely and store, covered, in the refrigerator for up to 3 days. Reheat before serving.

Oven-Barbecued Pork Ribs

I will be completely up front regarding barbecue: Unless you are willing to invest in a smoker or build a smoking pit out back, you really can't make genuine barbecue at home. This recipe, however, will get you mighty close to the real thing. It depends on long, slow cooking in a low oven for that characteristic, falling-off-the-bone tenderness of the meat, and on smoked paprika to impart the hickory flavor. Serve these ribs with my Barbecue Sauce (page 20), Old-Fashioned Coleslaw (page 91), Baked Beans (page 53), and New Potato Salad (page 95).

MAKES 2 MAIN-DISH SERVINGS

One 12-bone pork rib rack

Freshly ground black pepper

Smoked Spanish paprika

Barbecue sauce of your choice (page 20)

1. Bring the ribs to room temperature prior to cooking.
2. Preheat the oven to 200°F. Line a sheet pan with heavy-duty aluminum foil.
3. Rinse the ribs and pat it dry with paper towels. Place the slab, bone side down, on the prepared sheet pan and liberally season the ribs with the black pepper and paprika. Cover with another piece of heavy-duty foil, crimping it around the edges to seal tightly. Bake for 1 hour.
4. Reduce the oven temperature to 180°F and cook for 5 hours. Remove from the oven and turn on the broiler.
5. Carefully remove the top piece of foil from the ribs, as the steam can burn you, and liberally brush the upper surface of the ribs with the barbecue sauce. Return to the oven uncovered and broil for 3 to 5 minutes, until the sauce has glazed and the juices sizzle. Remove from the oven.
6. Using tongs, transfer the ribs to a work surface and slice it in half. Transfer the half slabs to 2 serving plates. Serve hot with additional barbecue sauce.

BARBECUE

If you want to start an argument in the South, claim that someone else's barbecue is better than the one you're currently eating. Around here, everybody makes the *best* barbecue. I don't intend to wade into the debate, because it's a contentious one that probably goes back centuries, to the first encounters between the Spanish explorers and Caribe Indians, who are credited with introducing Europeans to the technique.

In western North Carolina, whole-hog barbecue is the preferred style. In East Tennessee, Boston butt or pork shoulder roasts are by far the favorite, with pork ribs not far behind. While it's true that poultry, beef, sausages, and cheese (yes, cheese!) are also fodder for the barbecue, you encounter many fewer aficionados of them than you do of pork. Regardless of the species or cut of meat, "low and slow" cooking over indirect heat from a hickory-wood fire is the traditional method of cooking barbecue; in fact, it can take more than 12 hours to cook a really good pork shoulder.

What can one say about barbecue that has not already been said by someone else? People have been cooking meat over fire for millennia, so what could possibly be the big deal? The fact is that not just any piece of meat, not just any sort of fire, and not just a regular sort of cook will do. All of these factors have to come together in the right proportions to create really great barbecue. A pit master, who tends the fire and bastes and turns the meat as it cooks, develops his or her skill through observation and practice. It literally takes years to master the art of barbecue, just as with any other skilled craft.

Without even wading into the vast ocean of opinion regarding barbecue sauces, bastes, rubs, and other flavor enhancers, let me first assert that you probably can't produce really great barbecue at home. You can turn out some excellent imitations, but the real thing requires all the equipment and trouble you might imagine from my descriptions above.

Skillet-Braised Pork Chops with Onion Jam

Pork chops have long been a part of Appalachian cooking. Fried in lard or bacon fat, and breaded or not, chops can appear on a plate at any time of day. This stovetop braise lends itself to a special-occasion dinner for two. All you need is this, a green salad, a baked potato, and a glass of wine, and dinner is served. If you don't want to make the onion jam, or simply don't have time, you can find similar products in well-stocked grocery stores.

MAKES 2 MAIN-DISH SERVINGS

Two 4-ounce boneless pork loin chops

Pinch of sugar

Freshly ground black pepper

1 tablespoon bacon drippings

2 bay leaves

½ cup beef stock

⅓ cup heavy whipping cream

Salt

Onion Jam (page 27), for serving

Minced fresh flat-leaf parsley, for garnish

1. Bring the chops to room temperature prior to cooking.

2. Pat the chops dry with paper towels and sprinkle one side of each with the sugar and as much black pepper as you like.

3. Warm the bacon drippings in a large, heavy skillet with a lid over medium heat until they begin to ripple. Add the chops, sugar side down, and apply additional pepper to the top sides. Cook, undisturbed, for 4 minutes. Turn the chops, place 1 bay leaf on top of each, and cook for 4 minutes.

4. Preheat the oven to 200°F. Place 2 serving plates in the warm oven.

5. Pour the beef stock into the skillet and cook, scraping up any browned bits with a wooden spoon, for 1 minute. Reduce the heat to the lowest possible setting, cover, and braise as gently as possible for 15 minutes.

6. Remove the chops from the skillet and place them on the warmed serving plates. Return the chops and plates to the oven while you finish the dish.

7. Stir the cream into the liquid remaining in the skillet. Raise the heat to medium-high and bring to a boil. Reduce the heat to medium and cook, stirring ocassionally, for 5 to 7 minutes, or until the sauce has reduced to the desired consistency.

8. To serve, spoon a dollop of the Onion Jam on each chop and surround each chop with the pan sauce. Garnish the dish with the parsley and serve.

Roast Pork Tenderloin with Mustard Gravy

A whole pork tenderloin is a quick and easy way to get dinner on the table for guests. Prior to the days of refrigeration, pork tenderloin was canned using a pressure canner. Once the canned tenderloin was drained, the liquid was used to prepare a rich gravy. Here, we begin with a fresh, whole tenderloin cooked in the oven and make a pan gravy flavored with homemade mustard to complement it. Substitute Creole or Dijon mustard if you have not made your own.

MAKES 4 MAIN-DISH SERVINGS

FOR THE PORK TENDERLOIN:

Vegetable oil

2 tablespoons minced fresh rosemary

1 teaspoon freshly ground black pepper

½ teaspoon freshly ground white pepper

One 1- to 1½-pound whole pork tenderloin

¼ cup hot water

FOR THE GRAVY:

¼ cup rich pork or beef stock (see Note)

1 tablespoon Homemade Beer Mustard (page 16), Creole mustard, or Dijon mustard

1 tablespoon unsalted butter, cut into small pieces

Kosher salt

Note: You can make your own rich pork or beef stock by simmering ½ cup of homemade or canned stock until its volume is reduced by half. If using canned stock, choose a low-salt version.

1. Prepare the pork tenderloin: Preheat the oven to 400°F.

2. Lightly coat a heavy, ovenproof skillet with vegetable oil. Combine the rosemary and the black and white peppers on a sheet of waxed paper. Lightly oil the pork tenderloin and then roll it in the seasonings.

3. Place the prepared tenderloin in the skillet, add the water, and roast for 30 minutes, or until an instant-read thermometer inserted in the thickest part of the meat registers 145°F. Remove from the oven. Using metal tongs, transfer the tenderloin to a platter and tent with foil to keep warm. Turn off the oven and place 4 serving plates in it to warm.

4. Prepare the gravy: Place the skillet with its accumulated juices over medium heat. Add the stock and Homemade Beer Mustard and stir until fully incorporated. Bring to a simmer. Reduce the heat to low and slowly add the butter, a little at a time, stirring constantly to make sure each addition is fully incorporated before adding more. Remove from the heat, taste for seasoning, and adjust as needed.

5. Slice the pork and arrange it on the warmed serving plates. Drizzle with the mustard gravy and serve hot.

Peppercorn Pork Roast with Mornay Sauce

In this recipe, we bring together some of the best ingredients available in season. Walland, Tennessee's Blackberry Farm makes its "Under the Pines" cheese from its cows' winter milk and wraps it for aging with long pine needles that lend a slight hint of their fragrance to the finished product. If you can't find it, use any good aged Gruyère for the sauce. This would be a great dish to pair with French Bean and Sweet Corn Salad (page 59).

MAKES 4 MAIN-DISH SERVINGS

1 small (1-pound) pork tenderloin

2 tablespoons Dijon mustard

1 tablespoon black peppercorns

1 tablespoon white peppercorns

1 tablespoon green peppercorns

1 tablespoon pink peppercorns

2 tablespoons unsalted butter

1 tablespoon all-purpose flour

1 cup 2% milk

1 small onion studded with 2 whole cloves

1 ounce Under the Pines cheese or aged Gruyère, cut into small pieces

1 garlic clove, minced

Freshly ground black pepper, for garnish

Minced fresh rosemary, for garnish

1. Preheat the oven to 375°F. Pat the tenderloin dry and brush the mustard all over it.

2. Combine the peppercorns in a large mortar and pestle and coarsely grind them, or place them in a zip-top plastic bag and crush them with a heavy skillet. Spread the crushed peppercorns on a plate and roll the tenderloin in them, making sure to coat it on all sides. Transfer the pork to a rack over a baking sheet and roast for 1 hour, or until an instant-read thermometer inserted in the thickest part of the meat registers 145°F.

3. While the pork cooks, melt 1 tablespoon of the butter in a medium saucepan with a lid over medium-low heat. Add the flour, whisk until well combined, and cook for 1 minute. Add the milk and cook, whisking constantly, for 3 minutes, or until the sauce is smooth and thickened.

4. Reduce the heat to the lowest setting and add the clove-studded onion to the saucepan. Cover and gently simmer for 20 minutes. Remove and discard the onion. Add the cheese, the remaining 1 tablespoon of the butter, and the garlic, stirring con-

stantly until the cheese is melted. Cover and keep warm on the heat.

5.   When the tenderloin is done, remove it from the oven and transfer to a cutting board. Turn off the oven and place 4 serving plates in it to warm. Tent the tenderloin with foil and set aside to rest for 10 minutes.

6.   Slice the pork into medallions. Ladle a pool of the pan sauce into the center of each serving plate. Arrange equal portions of the medallions on top of the sauce on each plate. Garnish each plate with a few grinds of the black pepper and a pinch of the minced rosemary and serve.

Sausage Balls

A favorite at parties and potlucks, sausage balls can be made in advance. Freeze them on trays lined with waxed paper, then store in plastic freezer bags. Thaw overnight in the refrigerator before reheating in the oven at 350°F for 10 minutes. Country sausage is produced locally in several places in the southern mountains. We're partial to Swaggerty's, which is made in Kodak, Tennessee. Most brands are available in mild, hot, and sage varieties—use whichever one you prefer for this recipe.

MAKES 3 DOZEN

3 cups biscuit baking mix

1 pound country sausage, at room temperature

6 ounces freshly grated sharp Cheddar, at room temperature

6 ounces freshly grated aged Gouda, at room temperature

1. Preheat the oven to 400°F.
2. Combine all of the ingredients in a large mixing bowl and mix to form a dough-like consistency. If the mixture is too dry, add hot water, 1 teaspoon at a time, until it can be shaped.
3. Form the mixture into bite-size balls and space them out on an ungreased baking sheet. Bake for 12 to 15 minutes, or until golden brown. Remove from the oven.
4. Serve immediately. If storing, cool to room temperature and then place in an airtight container. Store in the freezer for up to 6 months.

Hog Jowl and Black-Eyed Peas

Traditionally eaten on New Year's Day, this combination of winter foods supposedly brings good luck to those who consume it. With an added helping of cooked greens, this dinner will bring prosperity, too. While I can't vouch for the effectiveness of these dishes in molding one's future, I can certainly do so in regard to their flavor. Smoked hog jowl may be hard to find outside the mountain regions of the South, so substitute thick-sliced smoked bacon if you must.

MAKES 4 TO 6 MAIN-DISH SERVINGS

1 cup dried black-eyed peas

1 pound smoked hog jowl, sliced ¼ inch thick

Chopped red onion

Hot sauce, for serving

1. Rinse the black-eyed peas in a colander. Transfer them to a bowl, cover with water, and soak overnight in the refrigerator.

2. Preheat the oven to 375°F and position a rack in the middle of the oven.

3. Place the hog jowl on a rack over a broiler pan in a single layer and bake for 15 minutes. Rotate the pan 180°, reduce the oven temperature to 350°F, and bake for 15 minutes. Rotate the pan 180° again and bake for 15 minutes. Remove from the oven and set aside to cool slightly on the rack. Reduce the oven temperature to 200°F.

4. Transfer the hog jowl to a platter and set aside.

5. Drain the black-eyed peas. Place them in a medium saucepan and cover with cold water. Chop 2 slices of the cooked hog jowl into small pieces and add them to the saucepan. Place the saucepan over medium-high heat and bring to a boil. Reduce the heat to medium-low, cover, and simmer for 1 hour, or until the peas are tender. Remove from the heat.

6. Shortly before the peas are done, place 4 to 6 serving plates in the warm oven.

7. When the peas are done, place a slice of hog jowl on each serving plate to warm. Ladle the peas onto the prepared plates and garnish each plate with the red onion. Serve with the hot sauce for guests to add as they wish.

Chicken and Dumplings

Many cooks prepare chicken and dumplings using rolled dough cut into strips. While that's a fine way to do it, this dropped version is a lot easier to master, and the result is a light, fluffy dumpling. A few flourishes added to this recipe also elevate this humble, comforting dish. This dish is traditionally made with meat from a hen that has outlived her egg-production days, but I recommend fresh chicken thighs instead; they're usually a bargain at the grocery store and offer a good balance of white and dark meat. But by all means, use a whole chicken if you prefer. If you have leftover chicken fat, use it to fry up some potatoes.

MAKES 8 MAIN-DISH SERVINGS

FOR THE CHICKEN:

3 to 4 pounds chicken thighs (with bones and skin)

6 cups water

½ cup finely diced celery

2 teaspoons salt

1 bay leaf

1 teaspoon dried or 1 tablespoon fresh oregano

½ teaspoon dried or 1½ teaspoons fresh thyme

¼ teaspoon freshly ground black pepper

FOR THE DUMPLINGS:

2 cups all-purpose flour

1 tablespoon baking powder

1 teaspoon salt

1 cup whole milk

Minced fresh flat-leaf parsley, for garnish

1. Prepare the chicken: Remove the skin and any masses of fat from the chicken pieces. Slice the skin into small pieces and place them, along with the fat, in a medium saucepan over medium-low heat.

2. Cook gently, stirring from time to time, for 30 minutes, or until all the fat has been rendered and the pieces of skin are golden and crisp. Strain the fat into a heatproof measuring cup and reserve it. Save the crispy chicken skin to garnish the finished dish. (The chicken skin and fat can be prepared up to this point 1 day in advance; if doing so, set them aside to cool to room temperature and then store them, covered, in the refrigerator. Bring to room temperature before proceeding with the recipe.)

3. Combine the chicken thighs and water in a large pot or Dutch oven with a lid over medium-high heat. When the water comes to a boil, reduce the heat to medium-low and skim off any foam that has risen to the surface. Continue skimming for a few minutes, or until little or no additional foam appears.

4. Add the celery, salt, bay leaf, oregano, thyme, and black pepper to the pot. Reduce the heat to low, cover, and cook at a slow simmer for 1 hour.

5. Using tongs, transfer the chicken to a plate to cool. Remove from the heat, remove and discard the bay leaf, and cover to keep the stock warm.

6. Once the chicken is cool enough to touch, debone it, reserving the meat and discarding the bones and trimmings. (The chicken can be prepared up to this point 1 day in advance; if doing so, store the boned chicken, covered, in the refrigerator. Plunge the pot containing the stock into a sink full of cold water to cool it rapidly. Then, transfer the stock to a covered container in the refrigerator as well.)

7. When you are ready to complete the recipe, measure the stock and add water as needed to bring the volume to 6 cups. Place the stock in a large pot or Dutch oven with a lid over medium-high heat and bring the stock to a simmer.

8. While the stock warms, make the dumplings: Combine the flour, baking powder, and salt in a mixing bowl. Measure out 3 tablespoons of the reserved chicken fat (if you don't have enough, use lard or vegetable shortening to make up the difference). Using a pastry blender, a fork, or your fingers cut the fat into the flour mixture until it resembles coarse meal. Add the milk, stirring with a few quick strokes to incorporate it and create a dough. Do not overmix—stir until just combined.

9. Raise the heat to high to bring the stock to a rolling boil. Drop the dumpling dough into the pot by teaspoonfuls (see Note). When all of the dough has been added, reduce the heat to medium-low, cover, and cook gently for 12 to 15 minutes—*do not uncover to check progress until 12 minutes have elapsed*—or until all of the dumplings are floating. Remove from the heat, taste for seasoning, and adjust as you deem appropriate.

10. Gently stir the reserved chicken meat into the pot. Ladle into bowls, garnish with the parsley and some of the reserved crispy chicken skin, and serve immediately.

Note: First, dip the teaspoon into the hot stock and then dip it again after each dumpling is added. This prevents the dough from sticking to the spoon.

Skillet-Fried Chicken with Gravy

Every Appalachian cook has a recipe for fried chicken, but most agree that brining and breading are the keys to getting the best flavor. Many turn to buttermilk for the overnight marinade, but a simple brine is easier *and* cheaper. Save the buttermilk for the biscuits, or add a little to the egg before breading the pieces of chicken. I got the idea to mix multiple fats from Sean Brock's cookbook, *Heritage*, but country cooks use whatever fat they have on hand.

MAKES 4 MAIN-DISH SERVINGS

8 cups cold water

½ cup kosher salt, plus more as needed

½ cup light brown sugar

4 chicken legs

12 chicken wing drumettes

2 cups plus 6 tablespoons all-purpose flour

2 teaspoons garlic powder

2 teaspoons plus 1 teaspoon freshly ground black pepper

½ teaspoon ground cayenne pepper or Highland Heat Seasoning (page 17)

4 cups plus ½ cup whole milk

2 large eggs

½ cup lard

½ cup rendered chicken fat

½ cup bacon drippings

¼ cup peanut oil

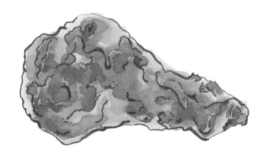

1. Prepare the brine by combining the water, salt, and sugar in a large container and stirring until the salt and sugar dissolve. Add the chicken and refrigerate overnight.

2. Remove the chicken from the brine, rinse each piece under cold water, and pat dry. Place on a plate lined with paper towels and return to the refrigerator. One hour before you are ready to fry, bring the chicken pieces to room temperature.

3. Combine 2 cups of the flour, the garlic powder, 2 teaspoons of the black pepper, and the cayenne in a large mixing bowl. Beat together ½ cup of the milk and the eggs in

a separate mixing bowl until the mixture is uniform.

4. Dip the chicken pieces, one at a time, in the milk mixture and then in the flour mixture. Return each piece to the milk mixture a second time, and then again to the flour mixture. Place the pieces on a rack to dry.

5. Preheat the oven to 200°F. Place a platter in the warm oven.

6. Combine the lard, chicken fat, bacon drippings, and oil in a large, heavy skillet with a lid and warm the fat until it registers 300°F on a deep-fry thermometer.

7. Carefully slip the chicken pieces into the skillet, taking care not to crowd the pan; cook in batches if necessary. Cook each piece for 5 minutes, and then turn, cover, and cook for 5 minutes. Uncover, turn again, and cook for 5 minutes, or until each of the pieces is golden brown. As each piece is done, place it on a rack to briefly drain. Once each piece has drained, place it on the platter warming in the oven. Continue until all the chicken pieces have been fried.

8. Transfer 4 tablespoons of the fat in the skillet to a small saucepan over medium-low heat. Add the remaining 6 tablespoons of flour and cook, stirring constantly, for 1 minute. Stir in the remaining 4 cups of milk and the remaining 1 teaspoon of black pepper and continue to cook, stirring, until smooth and thickened. Remove from the heat. Taste the gravy for seasoning and add salt as needed.

9. Serve the warm fried chicken with the gravy.

SEASONING CAST IRON

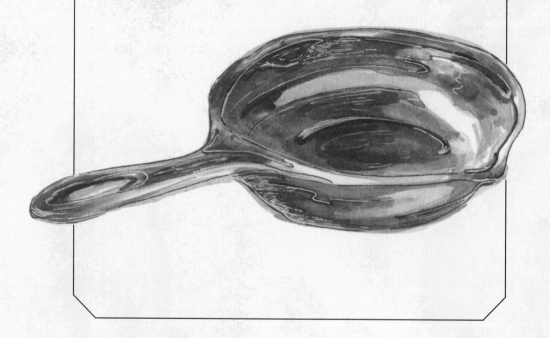

If, like me, you've inherited one or more pieces of well-seasoned cast-iron cookware, consider yourself a steward of fine cooking utensils that, with proper care, you can one day pass along to your descendants. Once seasoned, cast iron should never be cleaned with steel wool or harsh detergents, either of which may damage the layers of polymerized fats that create its nonstick surface. Instead, use warm water and a sponge to remove food residues; use only a a drop or two of mild detergent to help with grease. Always be sure not to scrub too hard when cleaning. Rinse thoroughly in cold water and dry completely before storage.

Oft-repeated warnings not to cook tomatoes or other acidic foods in cast iron are baseless—provided the utensil has been properly seasoned. The seasoning protects the iron from attack by food acids.

You can sometimes find good cast iron at flea markets and yard sales. As long as the skillet isn't warped—place it on a flat, level surface to check—you can restore it and use it for decades. If you get your hands on an old skillet, clean it thoroughly with soap and water, removing any rust with a scrub brush, and then season it again as if it were new.

To season a new skillet, coat it lightly all over with vegetable shortening and place it in the oven. Set the oven temperature to 350°F, turn it on, and bake for 1 hour. Turn off the oven and allow the skillet to cool completely inside the oven. Repeat this procedure monthly—assuming you use the skillet regularly—and soon the skillet will develop a proper nonstick patina. After three or four months, normal use should maintain the seasoned surface.

Care for a new skillet in the same way you would an older one. The nonstick properties of the skillet get better with each use, so bring it out often—especially when making the recipes in this book.

Indigenous Stew

I have no evidence that Native Americans made anything quite like this vegetable soup, which is made only with ingredients from the New World—I just thought the name would be fun because it's a bit of a tongue twister. This recipe was tested in the dead of winter, so I had to use frozen vegetables along with a zucchini that no doubt came a long way to get here. (You can always substitute winter squash or pumpkin.) The fresh tomatoes I used were produced in a greenhouse in western North Carolina; bred for the cooler mountain temperatures, they were remarkably tasty for such an unseasonable time of year. I look forward each August to making this stew with fresh vegetables at their seasonal peak. Serve with Easy or Heirloom Corn Bread (pages 34 and 35) and Pickled Ramps (page 10).

MAKES 2 MAIN-DISH SERVINGS OR 4 FIRST-COURSE SERVINGS

3 cups Turkey Stock (recipe follows)

1 medium potato

1 small zucchini

½ cup cut green beans, fresh or frozen

½ cup green baby lima beans, fresh or frozen

½ cup corn kernels, fresh or frozen and thawed

¼ cup wild rice

6 small tomatoes

Salt

Ground cayenne pepper

Reserved turkey meat from Turkey Stock recipe (optional)

2 tablespoons pepitas (pumpkin seeds), for garnish

1. Bring the Turkey Stock to a gentle boil in a large saucepan or soup pot over medium heat.

2. Peel the potatoes and cut them into ½-inch cubes.

3. Trim off and discard the ends of the zucchini. Stand the zucchini on one end and cut downward, lengthwise, to produce ½-inch-thick slices, each with the peel intact. Remove and discard the seeds and cut the zucchini into ½-inch cubes.

4. Add the potatoes and zucchini to the stock and cook until it returns to a simmer. Add all of the remaining vegetables, except the tomatoes, and the rice and cook until it returns to a simmer.

5. Reduce the heat to medium-low and cook, covered, for 15 minutes, or until the potatoes are tender (test a cube with the edge of a spoon to ensure they are done).

6. Core and chop the tomatoes. Add them to the stew and cook until it returns to a sim-

mer. Cook for 1 minute and then remove from the heat. Taste for seasoning and add the salt and as much of the cayenne pepper as you wish. If you are using the turkey meat, add it to the stew at this point.

7. Toast the pepitas in a small, heavy skillet over high heat for 1 to 2 minutes, or until one or two seeds pop, making sure to constantly stir and toss them to prevent burning. Remove from the heat. Transfer the pepitas to a heatproof bowl and set aside to cool for 1 minute.

8. Serve the stew in individual serving bowls garnished with the pepitas.

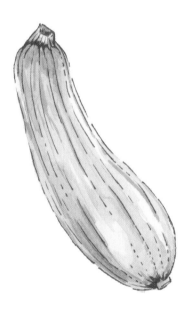

Turkey Stock

4 cups water

1 turkey leg

2 dried red pepper pods

¼ teaspoon salt

1. Combine the water, turkey leg, pepper pods, and salt in a large stockpot over medium heat and bring to a simmer. Cook for 45 minutes, occasionally skimming off and discarding any foam that rises to the top. Remove the leg with tongs and set it aside to cool slightly.

2. Using a sharp knife, separate the turkey leg's skin, meat, and bone. If you do not plan to use the meat, discard it; if you do, place it in a bowl and refrigerate until ready to use.

3. Return the turkey skin and bone to the stockpot and continue to simmer until the liquid's volume is reduced by a quarter. Remove from the heat and strain the stock, discarding any solids that remain.

4. Either use the stock immediately or, if making ahead, allow the stock to cool to room temperature, and then transfer to an airtight container and refrigerate. (To hasten the stock's cooling process, plunge the stockpot into a sink full of ice water.) Use within 3 days.

Tamales

An ancient Mayan dish, tamales were probably known in some form to the Mississippian and Catawba cultures that once inhabited the mountain South. No one seems to know why tamales are so popular in Knoxville. They're on the menu at many diners, and fancy versions can be found in food trucks devoted to them. Rural grocery stores often offer them, alongside bologna sandwiches, on the menu board. Apparently, tamales migrated here in modern times along with people from the Mississippi Delta region, where tamales have been a popular local food for generations. They're a bit of a production and are best made assembly-line style, so it's wise to enlist helpers. Read through the recipe carefully and decide in advance how you will prepare them. Tamales freeze well, so you can make a big batch and enjoy them over a long period of time—that's what most people do around here. Allow frozen tamales to thaw overnight in the refrigerator before steaming them for 10 minutes to reheat. They can also be reheated in the microwave.

MAKES 24 TAMALES, WITH LEFTOVER FILLING

24 corn husks

¼ cup Tamale Seasoning (page 18)

3 tablespoons vegetable oil

1 pound ground bison

1 pound ground turkey

1 medium onion, chopped

3 garlic cloves, minced

3 tablespoons chopped pickled jalapeño pepper

1 recipe Masa for Tamales (page 132)

1. Soak the corn husks in a large bowl filled with cold water for at least 30 minutes before filling them. If tying the tamales (see step 7), have a ball of cotton kitchen string handy, along with scissors.

2. Warm the oil in a large, heavy skillet over medium heat. Add the bison and turkey and cook, stirring constantly and breaking up any large chunks, for 10 minutes, or until the meat is no longer pink.

3. Add the onion and garlic and cook for 5 minutes. Add the jalapeño pepper and ¼ cup of the tamale seasoning and cook for 5 minutes. Taste for seasoning and add more of the seasoning mix, if you wish. Cook for 3 minutes. Remove from the heat and set aside to cool.

4. To assemble each tamale, take 1 corn husk from the water, allowing any excess water to drain back into the bowl, and spread it on a flat work surface. Spread 3 tablespoons of the Masa for Tamales in a rectangle in the center of the corn husk. Spread 2 tablespoons of the cooked meat mixture down the center of the masa.

5. Fold one side of the corn husk over, and then the opposite side. The folds should

be tight enough that the meat layer is fully enclosed by the masa layer.

6. Fold up the bottom of the packet, but leave the top open. Stack the packets, open end up, in a metal bowl, placing the fold against the side of the bowl to hold it in place. (You may need to tilt the bowl on its side until you have added several tamales, so they remain in place.) Use a folded kitchen towel to stabilize the bowl. Continue in this fashion until you have used all of the masa. Save the leftover cooked meat for making chili (see the Knoxville Full House recipe, page 133).

7. If the tamales do not remain upright, use a smaller metal bowl or a canning jar to keep them propped up. The open ends of the tamales must point upward during the steaming process to avoid losing the filling. (If this seems like a lot of trouble, consider the alternative: Fold down both ends of the tamales and tie them in both directions with kitchen string. They can then be stacked horizontally in a steamer basket.

It's totally your call, as the end result will be the same. Tying them seems like a lot of trouble to me, but if I had helpers, I might go that route.)

8. Place a trivet inside a stockpot large enough to hold the bowl of tamales above 1 inch or more of boiling water. Add the 1 inch of water and place over medium heat. If you lack a pot large enough to do this, tie the tamale packets and steam them using a basket and a saucepan; you can steam them in batches, if necessary. Keep the others refrigerated while you steam the first batch. Prepared tamales can be kept in the refrigerator for up to 3 days before steaming.

9. Steam each batch of tamales for 1 hour and 10 minutes, if they have been previously refrigerated, or 1 hour if they are at room temperature. Remove from the heat. Carefully remove the bowl or steamer basket from the pot.

10. Serve immediately or set the tamales aside to cool to room temperature before freezing them.

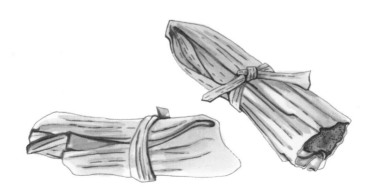

Masa for Tamales

Combined with additional ingredients and some elbow grease, *masa harina* is transformed into a light, fluffy component of homemade tamales. A stand mixer takes most of the work out of making masa. *Masa harina* is available in Latin American specialty markets and well-stocked supermarkets.

MAKES ENOUGH FOR 24 TAMALES

2 cups *masa harina*

2 teaspoons baking powder

1½ teaspoons salt

⅓ cup vegetable shortening

1½ cups warm beef stock

1. Combine the *masa harina*, baking powder, and salt in a large mixing bowl (with an electric mixer) or the bowl of a stand mixer fitted with the paddle attachment and mix until well combined.

2. Add the vegetable shortening to the bowl and mix, stopping and scraping down the sides as needed, until the mixture resembles coarse crumbs. Add the warm beef stock in a stream while the mixer continues to run. Increase the speed of the mixer as needed and beat the masa until it is light and fluffy. (Test by dropping a small amount from the tip of a spoon into a glass of water. It should float. If not, continue beating and test again.)

3. Store the masa in a sealed container in the refrigerator while you continue with the preparation of the tamale recipe.

Knoxville Full House

Two tamales topped with a generous serving of chili make a "Full House." The origins of this dish remain obscure, and you are unlikely to find it on offer anywhere but Knoxville. My personal theory is that the dish was inspired by the pinto beans and corn bread combo that people around here used to eat almost daily. Chili has beans, and tamales involve cornmeal. The meat and spices just make it better. In any case, the chili needs to be rich and spicy, as in this recipe. Top the bowl with some grated white Cheddar, and you have a "Full House with Snow on the Roof." Some people like oyster crackers or saltines with theirs.

MAKES 8 MAIN-DISH SERVINGS

1 teaspoon cumin seeds

2 tablespoons chili powder

1 tablespoon garlic powder

1 tablespoon onion powder

1 teaspoon salt, plus more as needed

1 teaspoon dried oregano

1 teaspoon dried basil

1 teaspoon dried thyme

½ teaspoon freshly ground black pepper, plus more as needed

1 tablespoon bacon drippings or vegetable oil

1 pound ground beef

1 large onion, chopped

2 teaspoons minced garlic

1 cup beef broth

One 15-ounce can diced tomatoes, undrained

One 15-ounce can pinto beans, drained and rinsed

16 Tamales (page 130)

Grated white Cheddar, for garnish (optional)

Oyster crackers or saltines, for serving (optional)

1. Toast the cumin seeds in a small, heavy skillet over medium-high heat until they are fragrant and lightly browned, making sure to constantly stir and toss the seeds to prevent burning. Remove from the heat.

2. Transfer the seeds to a heatproof bowl and set aside to cool to room temperature.

3. Grind the seeds in a spice grinder and then combine the ground cumin with the chili, garlic, and onion powders, salt, oregano, basil, thyme, and black pepper. Stir until thoroughly combined and set the seasoning mix aside.

4. Warm the bacon drippings in a Dutch oven or large saucepan with a lid over medium heat. When they begin to ripple, add the beef. Stir and cook, breaking up large chunks, for

Continued . . .

10 minutes, or until the beef is no longer pink. Add the chopped onion and cook, stirring occasionally, for 5 to 7 minutes, or until the onion is translucent and the beef is browned. Add the garlic and cook for 1 minute. Add the seasoning mix and cook, stirring constantly, for 3 minutes, or until the ingredients are fully coated with the seasoning.

5. Add the beef broth and stir to deglaze the pot. Reduce the heat to medium-low and simmer for 20 minutes.

6. Add the tomatoes and beans and simmer for 15 minutes. Remove from the heat and taste for seasoning; adjust as needed. Cover to keep the chili warm until ready to serve.

7. To serve, arrange 8 large soup bowls. Place two of the tamales in the bottom of each bowl and ladle some chili on top of each. Garnish with the cheese, if desired.

8. Serve immediately, passing the crackers, if using.

Duck Breasts with Berry Sauce

Ideal for an intimate dinner, duck breasts get the gourmet treatment in this recipe. Redolent with fresh herbs, the duck is finished with a sauce made of fruit preserves and the added kick of hot peppers. The rich flavors of this recipe pair especially well with New South Turnip Greens (page 80) and Blue Cornmeal Griddle Cakes (page 37).

MAKES 2 MAIN-DISH SERVINGS

1 tablespoon plus 1 teaspoon vegetable oil

1 small chipotle pepper in adobo sauce

¼ cup Merlot wine

1 cup blueberry, cherry, or blackberry preserves

2 boneless duck breast halves (with skin), each approximately 8 ounces

1 tablespoon fresh thyme leaves

1 teaspoon minced fresh rosemary leaves

½ teaspoon salt

¼ teaspoon freshly ground black pepper

1 tablespoon unsalted butter

1. Warm the 1 teaspoon of oil in a small saucepan over medium-low heat. Add the chipotle pepper along with some of the adobo sauce, and cook, stirring and breaking up the pepper with the edge of a spoon, for 1 minute. Add the wine and cook for 1 minute. Add the preserves, stir until well combined, and bring the mixture to a simmer.

2. Cook for 1 minute. Remove from the heat and cover to keep warm while you prepare the duck.

3. Preheat the oven to 200°F. Place 2 serving plates in the warm oven.

4. Wipe the duck breasts dry with paper towels. Combine the thyme, rosemary, salt, and black pepper in a small bowl and rub the seasoning mixture into the duck, using all of it and making sure to thoroughly coat the duck.

5. Warm the 1 tablespoon of oil and the butter in a large, heavy skillet over medium heat until it foams. When the foam subsides, add the duck breasts, skin side down, and cook for 5 minutes, or until the skin is a rich golden brown. Turn the breasts with a spatula and cook for 4 minutes, or until an instant-read thermometer inserted in the thickest part of the meat registers 145°F.

6. Transfer the duck breasts to the warmed serving plates, ladle the berry sauce over them, and serve immediately.

Stuffed Carolina Trout

Native brook trout populate many of the innumerable streams that flow down both sides of the Appalachian Mountains. Now protected, the fish at one time likely provided food for Cherokee and European families alike. Farmed rainbow trout now replace "brookies" on mountain menus. I devised this simple recipe to showcase the delicate flavor of the fish. Serve it with Succotash (page 43) on the side. You can easily increase the recipe to serve additional guests.

MAKES 2 MAIN-DISH SERVINGS

Two 4-ounce boneless trout fillets

1 lemon

4 cherry tomatoes, quartered

3 scallions, white and green parts, chopped

1 tablespoon chopped fresh flat-leaf parsley, plus more for garnish

1 tablespoon extra virgin olive oil

Salt

Freshly ground black pepper

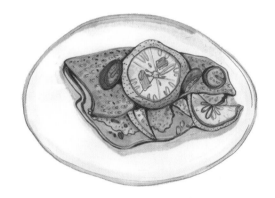

1. Preheat the oven to 350°F. Pat the trout fillets dry with paper towels and place them in an oiled shallow baking dish or in individual baking dishes.

2. Cut the lemon in half crosswise and pick out the seeds with the tip of the knife. Slice half of the lemon into thin slices and distribute them over the top of the trout fillets. Cut the remaining half into quarters to garnish the serving plates and reserve.

3. Place half the cherry tomatoes on top of the fillets, distributing them evenly. (Reserve the remaining tomatoes to garnish the plates.) Scatter the scallions over the fillets, followed by the parsley. Dribble the oil over the fish and vegetables and sprinkle them with a pinch or two of the salt and a few grinds of the black pepper.

4. Bake for 25 to 30 minutes, or until the fish flakes easily when pierced with a fork. If not using individual baking dishes, place serving plates in the oven to warm for the last 5 minutes of baking time. Remove from the oven and transfer the trout to the warmed serving plates, if using.

5. Garnish with the reserved lemon slices, tomatoes, and additional parsley and serve immediately.

SUNBURST TROUT FARMS

The rainbow trout (*Oncorhynchus mykiss*) is not native to the waters of the southern Appalachians, but it adapts superbly to aquaculture. Since 1948, Sunburst Trout Farms in Waynesville, North Carolina, has been cultivating rainbows using no antibiotics, hormones, or mammal-derived feed components in the pristine waters flowing from the Shining Rock Wilderness of Pisgah National Forest. Weighing as much as 2 pounds at harvest, trout from Sunburst is surely as close as we may be able to get to the flavor of the native mountain trout once enjoyed by both Native Americans and white settlers. Restaurants and specialty grocers in both eastern Tennessee and western North Carolina stock Sunburst products, or you can order them online (see Sources, page 183).

Simple Cornmeal Catfish

This method of preparing catfish may go all the way back to the Mississippian people, whose civilization was based on corn and stretched from the Atlantic seaboard all the way to just west of the Mississippi River. Fish was often fried in bear fat as a method of preservation, and a cornmeal coating may have helped improve the storage life of the finished product. This recipe is easily multiplied to serve more guests.

MAKES 2 MAIN-DISH SERVINGS

Two 4-ounce catfish fillets

¼ cup buttermilk

½ cup stone-ground yellow cornmeal

½ teaspoon salt

½ teaspoon Highland Heat Seasoning (page 17)

2 tablespoons vegetable oil

1. Place the catfish fillets in a shallow dish and pour the buttermilk over them. Turn the fillets to coat them and place the dish in the refrigerator until you are ready to cook.

2. Preheat the oven to 200°F. Place 2 serving plates in the warm oven.

3. Combine the cornmeal, salt, and Highland Heat Seasoning in a large, shallow dish, such as a pie pan. Remove the catfish from the refrigerator.

4. Warm the oil in a large cast-iron skillet over medium heat. Once the oil begins to ripple, dredge each fillet in the cornmeal mixture and slip it into the skillet. Cook for 3 minutes, or until lightly browned on the bottom. Flip with a spatula and cook on the other side for 3 minutes, or until lightly browned. Remove the catfish with a slotted spatula and set aside on a plate lined with paper towels to drain.

5. Transfer to the warmed serving plates and serve immediately.

THE BUFFALO FISH

Not long after the spring equinox, after a good, warm rain, certain rivers in the southern Appalachians host an unusual phenomenon. The black buffalo fish (*Ictiobus niger*) gather in enormous aggregations to spawn in the clear, clean waters of Citico Creek, the Ocoee River, and a few other locations in East Tennessee. Other fish species—notably the redhorse (*Moxostoma*) also have spring spawning runs.

Native Americans were well aware of these runs. They took advantage of the dense aggregations to net as many fish as they could, sometimes piling up rocks to create weirs to trap fish. Evidence dating back some 4,000 years to the Archaic period indicates the fish were cooked up right there on the creek bank. Cooked fish could be stored in woven grass sacks and taken back to the camps. Modern anthropological studies have revealed that the Cherokees determined when the spring fish runs would occur by paying attention to ecological signs, such as the blooming of blackberry bushes.

Hot-Dipped Catfish

Fried catfish is almost as ubiquitous on Appalachian tables as fried chicken. Several types of catfish occur naturally in the numerous rivers that drain the mountain slopes, but most of the catfish eaten around here now comes from farms in West Tennessee and Mississippi. Because of its distinctive but mild flavor and forgiving cooking qualities, catfish has enjoyed newfound popularity on Tennessee and North Carolina tables in recent years. This dish's breading is sturdier than that of the Simple Cornmeal Catfish recipe (page 138)—the breading holds the sauce without getting soggy. Serve this with Cucumber, Onion, and Tomato Salad (page 84) to tame the heat.

MAKES 2 MAIN-DISH SERVINGS

FOR THE CATFISH:

Two 4-ounce catfish fillets

½ cup all-purpose flour

½ cup stone-ground yellow cornmeal

1 tablespoon cornstarch

¼ teaspoon salt

Freshly ground black pepper

1 large egg

1 tablespoon whole milk

Oil for frying

FOR THE DIPPING SAUCE:

½ cup ketchup

1 cup white vinegar

1 tablespoon Homemade Hot Sauce (page 15) or your favorite store-bought hot sauce, or to taste

1. Prepare the catfish: Rinse the catfish fillets under cold water and pat dry with kitchen towels.

2. Combine the flour, the cornmeal, cornstarch, salt, and a few grinds of the black pepper in a wide, shallow bowl, stirring until well blended. Beat together the egg and milk in a separate bowl until the mixture is uniform.

3. Dip each catfish fillet, one at a time, in the flour mixture and make sure it is well coated. Then dip it in the egg mixture, making sure to let any excess moisture run off. Return each fillet to the flour mixture a second time. Place the catfish fillets on a platter lined with wax paper and store in the refrigerator until ready to cook.

4. Preheat the oven to 200°F. Place 2 serving plates in the warm oven.

5. Prepare the dipping sauce: Combine all of the ingredients in a small saucepan over

low heat and cook until piping hot. Remove from the heat but cover to keep warm while you cook the fish.

6. Warm ¼ inch of the oil in a large, heavy skillet over medium heat until it ripples. Carefully slip the catfish fillets into the oil and cook for 4 minutes, or until golden brown on the bottom. Flip with a spatula and continue cooking for 3 to 4 minutes, or until golden and crisp. Remove from the heat. Transfer the catfish fillets to a plate lined with paper towels to drain.

7. To serve, transfer the catfish to the warmed serving plates. Drizzle with some of the hot dipping sauce and serve immediately with the remaining sauce on the side.

Crawfish and Grits

The pristine streams of East Tennessee and western North Carolina host an abundance of life, including several species of crayfish (we say "crawfish"). No doubt these crustaceans formed part of the diet of indigenous people and early settlers alike. These days, crawfish come from farms in the Deep South, but that shouldn't prevent us from enjoying their unique, sweet flavor. Grocery stores sell pre-cooked crawfish, still in their bright red shells. You can substitute shrimp for the crawfish if you wish, but the flavor won't be as sweet.

MAKES 2 MAIN-DISH SERVINGS

2 pounds whole cooked crawfish in the shell

6 cups water, plus more as needed

2 celery ribs

2 shallots, peeled

1 garlic clove

1 bay leaf

¼ teaspoon black peppercorns

1 teaspoon Creole Three Seasoning (page 18)

¾ teaspoon salt

½ teaspoon Highland Heat Seasoning (page 17)

½ teaspoon dried basil

⅛ teaspoon dried thyme

½ cup yellow corn grits

2 tablespoons unsalted butter

1 tablespoon all-purpose flour

1 cup crawfish stock

2 scallions, finely chopped, for garnish

1 tablespoon finely chopped fresh flat-leaf parsley, for garnish

1. Peel the crawfish, reserving the tail meat in a bowl and placing the shells and heads in a medium saucepan (reserve 2 of the heads for garnishing the finished dish).

2. Add the water, 1 of the celery ribs, 1 of the shallots, the garlic, the bay leaf, and the peppercorns to the saucepan with the shells and place it over medium-high heat. Bring to a boil and skim off and discard any foam that rises to the top.

3. Mince the remaining celery rib and shallot and reserve for use in the sauce.

4. Reduce the heat to medium-low to maintain a steady simmer and cook the stock for 1 hour, or until the volume is reduced by half. Remove from the heat.

5. Strain the stock through a fine sieve and discard the solids. Measure out 1 cup of stock for the sauce and set it aside. Measure the remaining stock and add enough water as needed to make 2 cups, and set it aside.

6. Combine the Creole Three Seasoning, ¼ teaspoon of the salt, the Highland Heat

Seasoning, the basil, and the thyme in a small bowl and set the seasoning mix aside.

7. Bring the reserved 2 cups of stock and the remaining ½ teaspoon of the salt to a boil in a medium saucepan with a lid over high heat. Add the grits, stirring until well combined.

8. Reduce the heat to low, partially cover, and cook, stirring occasionally, for 15 to 20 minutes, or until the grits are creamy and smooth. Reduce the heat to the lowest setting and cover to keep warm.

9. Warm 1 tablespoon of the butter in a medium saucepan or Dutch oven with a lid over medium heat. Add 2 tablespoons each of the reserved minced shallots and celery and sauté for 1 minute, or until the shallot is translucent. Add the flour, stir well, and cook for 1 minute. Add the remaining 1 cup of reserved crawfish stock, pouring it in a consistent stream while stirring constantly, until the sauce is thickened and smooth. Add 1 teaspoon of the seasoning mix to the sauce, stir well, cook for 1 minute, and set the sauce aside. Reduce the heat to the lowest setting and cover to keep warm.

10. Preheat the oven to 200°F. Place 2 serving plates in the warm oven.

11. Melt the remaining 1 tablespoon of butter in a small skillet. Add the crawfish tails and 1 teaspoon of the seasoning mix and cook, tossing and stirring, for 3 minutes, or until the crawfish are warmed through.

12. To serve, ladle half of the grits into the center of one of the warmed serving plates. Top with half of the crawfish. Pour some of the sauce over the crawfish and garnish with the scallions, parsley, and the remaining seasoning mix. Decorate each plate with one of the reserved crawfish heads. Serve immediately.

Prosciutto-Wrapped Carolina Shrimp with Creamed Asparagus

Good enough for a special dinner, this recipe combines salty, umami-laden Tennessee prosciutto with plump, succulent Carolina shrimp and rich cream for an over-the-top entrée that's easy to prepare. If asparagus isn't in season, substitute freshly shelled green peas or thawed frozen peas, and give them the same brief steaming. Tennessee prosciutto is available by mail order (see Sources, page 183), but Italian prosciutto may be substituted. I like to serve this with a simple cucumber salad.

MAKES 2 MAIN-DISH SERVINGS

FOR THE VEGETABLES AND SHRIMP:

½ pound fresh asparagus, trimmed

Twelve 21- to 30-count Carolina shrimp

½ teaspoon Creole Three Seasoning (page 18)

⅛ teaspoon Highland Heat Seasoning (page 17)

3 paper-thin prosciutto slices

2 tablespoons unsalted butter

½ cup Shrimp Stock (recipe below)

½ cup heavy whipping cream

Mushroom Catsup (page 21), for serving

Minced fresh flat-leaf parsley, for garnish

Smoked Spanish paprika, for garnish

FOR THE SHRIMP STOCK:

Reserved shells from shrimp

½ cup chopped onion

½ cup chopped celery

½ cup chopped carrots

1 bay leaf

6 whole peppercorns

1. Prepare the vegetables and shrimp: Place a large pot with a steamer insert over medium-high heat. Add 1 inch of water to the pot and bring the water to a boil. Add the asparagus and steam for 6 minutes. Remove from the heat. Drain the asparagus into a colander and rinse under cold water to stop the cooking process. Drain well and reserve.

2. Peel and devein the shrimp, reserving the shells in a small saucepan and arranging the shrimp on a tray lined with paper towels. Place the tray in the refrigerator. Refrigerate the shells as well if it will be more than 30 minutes before you prepare the shrimp stock.

3. Prepare the shrimp stock: Add enough water to the saucepan to completely cover the shells. Add the ingredients for the shrimp stock to the saucepan and place it over medium heat. Bring to a boil.

4. Reduce the heat to low, so the liquid barely simmers, and cook for 1 hour. Strain out and discard the solids and return the stock to the saucepan over medium heat. Boil gently for about 20 minutes, or until its volume is reduced by half. Remove from the heat. (The stock can be prepared up to this point several days in advance; if doing so, cool it to room temperature and then store it, covered, in the refrigerator. Bring to room temperature before proceeding with the recipe.)

5. Combine the Creole Three Seasoning and Highland Heat Seasoning in a small bowl. Sprinkle the mixture over the shrimp, turning them to ensure the spices are evenly distributed. Tear each slice of prosciutto into 4 smaller pieces and use them to wrap each shrimp, folding the prosciutto around the thicker end. Return the shrimp to the refrigerator until you are ready to complete the dish. (This step can be prepared up to this point several hours in advance; if doing so, store the wrapped shrimp, covered, in the refrigerator.)

6. Preheat the oven to 200°F. Place 2 serving plates in the warm oven.

7. Melt 1 tablespoon of the butter in a large skillet over medium-low heat. When the foam subsides, add the shrimp and cook for 3 minutes. Turn each shrimp and continue cooking for 3 to 4 minutes, or until the shrimp are done and the prosciutto is crisp. Remove from the heat. Using tongs, evenly distribute the shrimp among the warmed serving plates. Return the plates to the oven.

8. Add ½ cup of the reduced shrimp stock and the heavy cream to the skillet used to cook the shrimp. Bring to a boil and cook for 3 minutes, or until slightly reduced and well blended. Remove the pan from the heat and cover it to keep warm.

9. Melt the remaining 1 tablespoon of butter in a small skillet. Add the asparagus and toss until it is well coated and heated through.

10. Remove the plates from the oven. Ladle some of the sauce over the shrimp and add the asparagus to 1 side of each plate. Dribble a few drops of the Mushroom Catsup into the sauce. Garnish the plate with a sprinkling of minced parsley and dust some of the paprika over the shrimp. Serve immediately.

Chapter Five

SWEET THANGS

It's no secret that Southerners like their sweets. Even when refined sugar was scarce, mountain folks used honey and sorghum in desserts, along with various wild and domesticated fruits. With the advent of railroads in the mid-nineteenth century, sugar from the coastal lowlands became more widely available in the mountains. Modern cooks continue to turn out pies, cakes, and cobblers from recipes their grandmothers recorded. Church cookbooks throughout the region always feature a selection of sweets, with Apple Stack Cake (page 148), Banana Pudding (page 152), and Vinegar Pie (page 156) frequently included.

Apple Stack Cake

An iconic Appalachian dessert, apple stack cake requires some effort, but it will reward you with intense apple flavor that permeates the cake layers. While traditional recipes yield a 9-inch cake, this 6-inch one is scaled down to four servings. The recipe is simple, but there are a couple of rules. Start with dried apples. Don't try to make the cake with applesauce or apple butter. The cake layers must be baked individually. You can't make them like pancakes on top of the stove, nor will you get the same result if you bake thicker layers and split them crosswise. Having a pair of small cast-iron skillets speeds things along, but you can bake the cake layers in any suitable pan. The layers will come out like soft, chewy cookies. The dough remains refrigerated while each layer bakes, so you can, if you wish, stretch the process across an afternoon. It is imperative that the cake sit for at least 24 hours before it is cut, and up to 3 days is fine, too. Read over the recipe carefully and plan your strategy before you begin; this cake is a good weekend project. The recipe for Oven-Dried Apples (page 23) should yield enough for this cake.

MAKES 4 SERVINGS

FOR THE FILLING:

4 ounces dried apples

¼ teaspoon ground cinnamon

¼ cup light brown sugar

FOR THE CAKE:

1½ cups all-purpose flour, plus more as needed

¼ teaspoon baking soda

⅛ teaspoon salt

¼ cup granulated sugar

2 tablespoons unsalted butter, at room temperature

2 tablespoons light brown sugar

2 tablespoons sorghum syrup

1 large egg, at room temperature

3 tablespoons buttermilk, at room temperature

¼ teaspoon vanilla extract

1.   Prepare the filling: Place the apples in a medium saucepan and cover them with cold water. Place the pan over high heat and bring to a boil.

2.   Reduce the heat to medium-low and simmer gently for 1 hour, or until the apples are very tender and most of the liquid has evaporated (stir occasionally near the end of the cooking time to prevent sticking). Remove from the heat.

3.   Add the brown sugar and cinnamon to the saucepan and stir and mash with a fork or potato masher until a uniform, jam-like mixture that retains a few larger pieces forms. Set aside. (The filling can be prepared up to this point 3 days in advance; if doing

so, store it, covered, in the refrigerator and bring to room temperature before proceeding with the recipe.)

4. Prepare the cake: Preheat the oven to 350°F. Spray one or more 6-inch cast-iron skillets with cooking spray and dust them liberally with flour (take care to do this thoroughly to prevent the cakes from sticking).

5. Combine the flour, baking soda, and salt in a large mixing bowl and stir with a fork until well combined.

6. Cream together the sugar and butter in a second mixing bowl until well combined. Stir in the brown sugar and sorghum syrup and beat until thoroughly combined.

7. Beat together the egg, buttermilk, and vanilla in a third mixing bowl until a uniform mixture forms.

8. Add a quarter of the flour mixture to the bowl containing the sugar mixture and mix with a large spoon until well combined. Add a third of the buttermilk mixture to the same bowl, mixing with the spoon until well combined. Add another quarter of the flour mixture, followed by another third of the buttermilk mixture, mixing until well combined with each addition. (It's best to mix the dough with a large spoon rather than an electric mixer, as you do not want to toughen the cake by working the dough too much.) Repeat with the remaining portions of the flour and buttermilk mixtures; the dough should hold together like cookie dough. If not, add more flour, 1 teaspoon at a time, and continue to mix gently until the consistency is right.

9. Turn out the dough on a floured work surface. Using a pastry blade or sharp knife, divide the dough into five equal portions. With your well-floured hands, form one or more portions into a flattened disk and then pat it gently into one of the skillets. Repeat for each skillet you have prepared; cover the remainder of the dough with a kitchen towel and refrigerate.

10. Place the prepared skillet(s) in the oven and bake for 11 minutes, or until golden brown.

11. As each layer is baked, remove from the oven and set aside to cool for 5 minutes. Run a spatula or a thin blade around the edge of the cake to free it and then carefully turn it out on a rack to cool for 5 minutes.

12. Transfer the first baked layer to a serving plate and spread a quarter of the filling on top of the cake layer. Top with another layer and repeat the process as each layer is baked, using one fourth of the filling each time and ending with a cake layer on top.

13. As needed, allow the skillets to cool before returning them to the oven. Rinse and dry them before spraying with cooking spray and flouring for the next layer.

14. When the cake is assembled, set it aside to cool completely.

15. Wrap the cake and serving plate in three layers of plastic wrap and set aside at room temperature for at least 24 hours, and up to 3 days, before slicing and serving.

16. Store any leftovers in the refrigerator and consume within 3 days.

Pineapple Upside-Down Cake

This cake became very popular in the 1920s, but it's related to other fruit cakes with a much longer history. While this cake *can* be made with fresh pineapple, canned pineapple is typically called for in recipes, as it was much more readily available a generation ago. If you don't have a cast-iron skillet of the proper size, a cake pan will do, but you may need to adjust the cooking time. Determine the cake's doneness using a thermometer, if that's the case. An electric mixer will make mixing the batter easier, but it can also be done by hand.

MAKES ONE 9-INCH ROUND CAKE

FOR THE TOPPING:

4 tablespoons (½ stick) unsalted butter, room temperature

¾ cup light brown sugar

6 canned pineapple rings

¼ cup chopped walnuts

FOR THE CAKE:

1¾ cups all-purpose flour

1½ teaspoons baking powder

½ teaspoon salt

8 tablespoons (1 stick) unsalted butter, room temperature

¾ cup granulated sugar

2 large eggs, room temperature

1½ teaspoons vanilla extract

½ cup pineapple juice, room temperature

1. Prepare the topping: Preheat the oven to 350°F.
2. Melt the butter in a 9-inch cast-iron skillet over medium-low heat. Remove from the heat and stir in the brown sugar, making sure the bottom is evenly coated. Place one of the pineapple rings in the center of the bottom of the skillet and surround it with the others. Fill in the center of each slice with the walnuts. Set aside while you prepare the batter.
3. Prepare the cake: Whisk together the flour, baking powder, and salt in a medium mixing bowl until well combined.
4. Cream the butter in a large mixing bowl until smooth. Add the sugar and beat for 4 minutes, or until the mixture is light and fluffy. Add the eggs, one at a time, mixing each one until it is fully combined. Beat in the vanilla extract.
5. Add a quarter of the flour mixture to the bowl containing the butter mixture and mix with a large spoon until well combined. Add a third of the pineapple juice to the same bowl, mixing with the spoon until well combined. Add another quarter of the

flour mixture, followed by another third of the juice, mixing until well combined with each addition. Repeat with the remaining portions of the flour mixture and juice; once you add the last of the flour mixture, beat for 1 minute, or until the dough is smooth.

6. Pour the batter into the prepared skillet and bake for 45 minutes to 1 hour, or until a tester inserted into the center of the cake comes out clean or an instant-read thermometer inserted in the thickest part of the cake registers 195°F. Remove from the oven and set aside on a rack to cool.

7. When it is cool enough to touch, run a knife around the edge of the skillet to free the cake from the sides. Invert a large plate over the skillet and, while holding the plate in place, flip over the skillet so the plate is on the bottom. Set the plate and skillet on the counter for a minute or two and the cake should slide right out onto the plate.

8. Allow the cake to cool to room temperature before attempting to slice it.

Banana Pudding

Too many people make banana pudding with a boxed pudding mix from the grocery store. On the other hand, I find separating eggs and whisking meringue to be more difficult as I have grown older, and a lot of old recipes call for that. This recipe uses whole eggs in the pudding, and store-bought marshmallow crème for the topping instead of the classic meringue; the idea for using marshmallow crème came from Chef Matt Gallagher of the Knox Mason restaurant in Knoxville. If you prefer, the pudding can be placed in individual ramekins rather than one large bowl.

MAKES 6 TO 8 SERVINGS

2½ cups whole milk

¾ cup minus 1 teaspoon granulated sugar

⅓ cup minus 1 teaspoon all-purpose flour

Pinch of salt

2 large eggs

1 teaspoon vanilla extract

3 bananas

Vanilla wafers

One 7-ounce jar marshmallow crème

1. Combine the milk, sugar, flour, and salt in a medium saucepan over medium-low heat and cook, stirring constantly, for 13 minutes, or until smooth and thickened.

2. Lightly beat the eggs in a medium mixing bowl.

3. Add ¼ cup of the hot mixture to the eggs to temper them (gradually raise their temperature) and then stir the contents of the mixing bowl into the saucepan.

4. Reduce the heat to low and cook, stirring constantly, for 3 minutes, or until thickened. Add the vanilla extract. Remove from the heat and set aside to cool slightly.

5. Place a layer of the vanilla wafers in the bottom of a large Pyrex bowl. Add a layer of the warm pudding, followed by a layer of bananas and another layer of pudding. Continue the layers until you have used all of the pudding, ending with the pudding on top. Spread the marshmallow crème over the surface of the pudding, sealing it at the edges, and refrigerate until ready to serve (optimally, overnight).

6. When ready to serve, set the bowl under the broiler for 3 to 4 minutes, or until the marshmallow crème is lightly browned on top. Remove from the oven and serve immediately.

Blackberry Crumble

Wild blackberries grow all over the mountains, and berry picking used to be a popular outdoor adventure for the whole family. Nowadays, most people get their berries from the farmers' market or grocery store, but plenty of wild ones still await the intrepid forager each July. This recipe is my favorite way to use leftover biscuits. You can also make this with frozen blackberries.

MAKES 2 SERVINGS

2 cups fresh blackberries

1 cup granulated sugar

1 whole clove

2 leftover Easy Buttermilk Biscuits (page 172)

2 teaspoons unsalted butter, plus more for greasing

Fresh whipped cream or ice cream, for serving

1. Combine the blackberries, sugar, and clove in a small saucepan, mashing a few of the blackberries with a spoon to release their juices. Place over medium heat and cook, stirring occasionally, for about 8 minutes, or until the sugar is dissolved and the mixture is bubbling and thickened (watch carefully, and don't allow it to become too thick). Remove from the heat and remove and discard the clove. Set aside.

2. Preheat the oven to 350°F. Butter two 1-cup ovenproof ramekins.

3. Crumble one of the biscuits into the bottom of each ramekin. Spoon equal portions of the blackberry mixture over each one, and top each with 1 teaspoon of the butter. Bake for 10 minutes. Remove from the oven.

4. Serve hot with the fresh whipped cream or ice cream.

Lemon Pie

My grandmother made this luscious pie to perfection. This recipe is as close as I have come to copying hers. Use only freshly squeezed lemon juice and freshly grated zest. I generally rely on store-bought pie crust, but you can also make your own from the recipe on page 161.

MAKES ONE 9-INCH PIE

4 large eggs, separated

¼ cup granulated sugar

¼ teaspoon cream of tartar

1½ cups granulated sugar

⅓ cup cornstarch

Large pinch of salt

1½ cups water

½ cup freshly squeezed lemon juice

1 tablespoon finely minced lemon zest

4 tablespoons (½ stick) unsalted butter, cut into small pieces

One 9-inch pie shell, baked and cooled

1. Preheat the oven to 350°F and position a rack in the center of the oven.

2. Beat together the egg whites, sugar, and cream of tartar in a medium mixing bowl until the mixture holds stiff peaks. Set the meringue aside.

3. Combine the sugar, cornstarch, salt, water, lemon juice, and lemon zest in a medium saucepan, stirring with a wire whisk until the sugar is mostly dissolved. Add the egg yolks, one at a time, stirring until each is completely incorporated. Add the butter and place the pan over medium heat. Cook, stirring constantly, for 15 minutes, or until the mixture is very thick.

4. Pour the pudding into the pie shell and top with the meringue, sealing at the edges. Bake for 10 to 15 minutes, or until lightly browned on top. Remove from the oven and set aside to cool to room temperature.

5. Slice and serve the pie at room temperature or chilled.

Atlantic Beach Pie Variation

When you bake my Lemon Pie (previous recipe) in a crust made from saltine cracker crumbs, you have an "Atlantic Beach Pie."

MAKES ONE 9-INCH PIE

70 saltine crackers

¼ cup granulated sugar

8 tablespoons (1 stick) plus 1 tablespoon unsalted butter, room temperature

4 large eggs, separated

¼ cup granulated sugar

¼ teaspoon cream of tartar

1½ cups granulated sugar

⅓ cup cornstarch

Large pinch of salt

1½ cups water

½ cup freshly squeezed lemon juice

1 tablespoon finely minced lemon zest

4 tablespoons (½ stick) unsalted butter, cut into small pieces

Pink Himalayan sea salt (optional)

1. In a large mixing bowl, crush the crackers with your hands until coarse crumbs form (the crackers should not be pulverized). Add the sugar and mix well. Add the room temperature butter, working it into the crumbs using a spoon or your hands, until a dough that holds together forms.

2. Press the mixture into a 9-inch pie tin or dish, taking care to build it up on the sides.

Place in the refrigerator to chill for at least 1 hour.

3. Preheat the oven to 350°F and position a rack in the center of the oven.

4. Bake the crust for 18 minutes, or until it is golden brown. Remove from the oven and set aside to cool to room temperature before filling.

5. Beat together the egg whites, sugar, and cream of tartar in a medium mixing bowl until the mixture holds stiff peaks. Set the meringue aside.

6. Combine the sugar, cornstarch, salt, water, lemon juice, and lemon zest in a medium saucepan, stirring with a wire whisk until the sugar is mostly dissolved. Add the egg yolks, one at a time, stirring until each is completely incorporated. Add the small pieces of butter and place the pan over medium heat. Cook, stirring constantly, for 15 minutes, or until the mixture is very thick.

7. Pour the pudding into the pie shell and top with the meringue, sealing at the edges. Bake for 10 to 15 minutes, or until lightly browned on top. Remove from the oven and set aside to cool to room temperature.

8. Decorate the finished pie with a sprinkle of the pink salt on top of the meringue, if you wish. Slice and serve the pie at room temperature or chilled.

Vinegar Pie

The Clinch Mountain Restaurant in Grainger County, Tennessee, is famous for its breathtaking views as well as its vinegar pie. Lacking more exotic flavorings, Appalachian cooks made do with vinegar as the acid note in this sweet-and-sour filling. The restaurant adds lemon extract to its pie, but I wanted a different take, so I substituted my Homemade Basil Vinegar. Experiment with different types of vinegars, and if you want to add lemon extract, use ½ teaspoon.

MAKES ONE 9-INCH PIE

FOR THE CRUST:

18 graham crackers (⅔ of a 14.4-ounce box)

⅓ cup granulated sugar

8 tablespoons (1 stick) unsalted butter, melted

FOR THE FILLING:

1 cup granulated sugar

1 cup water

2 tablespoons cornstarch

2 large eggs, well beaten

2 tablespoons Homemade Basil Vinegar (recipe follows) or other vinegar

1 tablespoon unsalted butter

Whipped cream, fresh fruit, or fruit preserves, for serving

1. Prepare the crust: Preheat the oven to 350°F.
2. Pulverize the graham crackers, using a rolling pin or a food processor and transfer the crumbs to a large mixing bowl. Add the sugar and stir until well combined. Drizzle the melted butter over the crumbs and stir until all the crumbs are fully coated.
3. Press the mixture into a 10-inch tart pan with a removable bottom; take care to press the mixture up the sides.
4. Place the pan on a baking sheet and bake for exactly 8 minutes. Remove from the oven and set aside on a rack to cool to room temperature.
5. Prepare the filling: Bring ½ inch of water to a simmer in the bottom part of a double boiler over medium heat.
6. Combine the sugar, water, and cornstarch in the top part of the double boiler and stir until the cornstarch dissolves. Add the eggs and vinegar and place the top part of the double boiler over the simmering water. Cook, stirring occasionally, for 30 minutes, or until thickened and smooth.

Stir in the butter until it has completely melted and is fully incorporated. Remove from the heat.

7. Pour the filling into the prepared crust.

Set aside to cool to room temperature and then refrigerate overnight before slicing.

8. Slice and serve the pie topped with whipped cream, fresh fruit, or fruit preserves.

Homemade Basil Vinegar

MAKES 1 PINT

2 cups rice vinegar

4 cups loosely packed, freshly picked basil leaves (preferably a purple-leaf variety; see Note)

1. Wash a 1-quart canning jar in hot, soapy water and rinse it thoroughly. Combine the vinegar and 2 cups of the basil leaves in the jar. Using a wooden spoon, press down on the leaves, bruising them slightly and ensuring that all are submerged. Place the jar in the refrigerator for 2 weeks.

2. Strain the vinegar through a sieve into a bowl and discard the solids. Wash the jar in hot, soapy water and rinse it thoroughly. Return the vinegar, along with another 2 cups of fresh basil leaves, to the jar. Using a wooden spoon, press down on the leaves, bruising them slightly and ensuring that all are submerged. Place the jar in the refrigerator for 2 weeks.

3. Strain the vinegar through a sieve into a bowl and discard the solids. Store the vinegar in a tightly sealed bottle in the refrigerator and use within 6 months.

Note: Since the basil leaves are used in two steps two weeks apart, you will need to pick or purchase separate batches for this recipe.

Green Tomato Pie

The filling for this pie demonstrates the ingenuity of the mountain people in using up everything from the garden in one way or another. When I first learned this recipe, I was struck by how much the filling resembles a chutney. I generally purchase refrigerated pastry crust, but you can also make your own from the recipe on page 161. Try serving a slice of this pie with a dollop of sweetened ricotta cheese.

MAKES ONE 9-INCH PIE

1 unbaked double-crust 9-inch pie crust pastry

1½ pounds green tomatoes

½ cup light brown sugar

½ cup chopped raisins

3 tablespoons unsalted butter, melted

2 tablespoons apple cider vinegar

½ teaspoon ground cinnamon

½ teaspoon salt

¼ teaspoon ground mace

⅛ teaspoon ground cloves

1. Preheat the oven to 375°F. Line a pie dish with half of the pastry; refrigerate it and the remaining pastry while you make the filling.

2. Core and coarsely chop the tomatoes. Measure out 2 cups of the chopped tomatoes (reserving the remainder for another use) and place them in a medium saucepan. Cover the tomatoes with cold water and place over high heat. Bring to a rapid boil and boil for 10 seconds. Remove from the heat and drain the tomatoes into a colander.

3. Transfer the tomatoes to a large mixing bowl, add the remaining ingredients, and stir until well combined.

4. Turn out the filling into the prepared crust. Top the pie with the second crust, trimming and folding the edges under. Crimp the edge to seal the crust and then make several slashes in the top to permit steam to escape. Place the pie on a baking sheet and bake for 35 minutes, or until the top is golden brown. Remove from the oven and set aside to cool completely.

5. Slice and serve.

Chocolate Pie

This is a dish straight from my mama's kitchen. Long before there were boxed pie fillings, Southern moms were stirring up this thick chocolate pudding. Good-quality pastry crust can be found in the refrigerated case at the grocery, or you can also make your own from the recipe on page 161.

MAKES ONE 9-INCH PIE

1¼ cups granulated sugar

½ cup unsweetened cocoa powder

3 tablespoons all-purpose flour

¼ teaspoon salt

2 cups whole milk

2 large eggs, separated

2 tablespoons unsalted butter, melted

½ teaspoon vanilla extract

One 9-inch pie shell, baked and cooled

¼ teaspoon cream of tartar

1. Combine 1 cup of the sugar, the cocoa powder, flour, and salt in a medium saucepan. Add the milk, stirring until thoroughly combined; in particular, make sure that all of the flour is completely incorporated.

2. Place the saucepan over medium heat and cook, stirring for 15 minutes, or until thickened.

3. Thoroughly beat the egg yolks in a mixing bowl. Add ¼ cup of the hot chocolate mixture to the yolks to temper them (gradually raise their temperature) and then stir the contents of the mixing bowl into the saucepan.

4. Reduce the heat to medium-low and cook gently, stirring constantly, for 3 minutes. Stir in the butter and vanilla extract and remove from the heat.

5. Pour the custard into the prepared pie shell and set aside to cool.

6. Beat together the egg whites, the remaining ¼ cup of the sugar, and the cream of tartar in a medium mixing bowl until the mixture holds stiff peaks. Set the meringue aside.

7. When the pie has completely cooled, cover the top with the meringue. Chill until you are ready to serve.

8. When ready to serve, set the pie under the broiler for 3 to 4 minutes, or until lightly browned on top. Remove from the oven, slice, and serve immediately.

Chocolate Whiskey Pecan Pie

Pecan pie probably evolved from chess pie and similar egg and sugar concoctions as inventive cooks began to add seasonally available nuts. Eventually, when big, sweet hybrid pecans became widespread, they ended up becoming the nut of choice. Instead of the pecans, you can try English walnuts in the filling. If you can find them, black walnuts, wild pecans, and hickory nuts produce a result more like what would have been enjoyed by mountain families who gathered nuts every autumn. Make your own pie crust from the recipe on the following page, or purchase one at the market, as I often do.

MAKES ONE 9-INCH PIE

1 unbaked single-crust 9-inch pie crust pastry

¾ cup sorghum syrup

⅓ cup dark brown sugar

2 large eggs, well beaten

4 tablespoons (½ stick) unsalted butter, melted

1½ ounces Tennessee whiskey

1½ teaspoons pure vanilla extract

¼ teaspoon salt

1½ cups chopped pecans

1½ ounces semi-sweet chocolate, freshly grated

⅓ cup pecan halves, for topping

1. Preheat the oven to 400°F.

2. Line a 9-inch pie pan with the pastry pie crust, attractively trimming and fluting the edges. Line the pastry with parchment paper, fill with pie weights, and bake for 10 minutes.

3. Remove the pie weights and parchment paper and bake for 2 minutes. Remove from the oven and set aside on a rack to cool. Reduce the oven temperature to 350°F.

4. Combine the sorghum syrup, brown sugar, eggs, melted butter, whiskey, vanilla and salt, and set aside.

5. Sprinkle the pecans and chocolate on the bottom of the pie shell and spread the sorghum mixture on top of them. Garnish the top with the pecan halves in a decorative arrangement and bake for 30 to 45 minutes, or until golden brown and set. Remove from the oven and transfer to a wire rack to cool for 2 hours or more before slicing.

6. Slice and serve.

Pie Crust

Frozen or refrigerated pie crust from the grocery is a great time saver, but you can also make a good pie crust at home. A food processor makes short work of combining the flour and fat.

MAKES 1 DOUBLE-CRUST 9-INCH PIE

1 cup all-purpose flour

⅛ teaspoon salt

8 tablespoons (1 stick) unsalted butter, cut into cubes

3 tablespoons ice water

1. Place the flour, salt, and butter in the bowl of a food processor. Chill the bowl and ingredients for at least one hour in the refrigerator before continuing with the recipe.

2. Remove the bowl from the refrigerator and process for about 10 seconds to incorporate the butter into the flour. With the motor running, add the water, a tablespoon at a time, until the dough comes together in a ball.

3. Transfer the dough to a floured work surface and knead a few times until it is smooth. Form the dough into a disk about an inch thick, wrap in plastic wrap, and refrigerate for at least 1 hour. The dough may be made a day ahead and stored in the refrigerator overnight.

4. Remove the dough from the refrigerator and allow it to warm up for 5 minutes. Divide the dough in half and roll it out on a floured surface until it is about ⅛-inch thick. Prebake or fill and bake as directed in individual recipes.

Persimmon Pudding

Native persimmons have been feeding people since prehistoric times. The ripe persimmons must be gathered after a frost, or they won't be edible. There's no substitute for them in this recipe, which is over a century old. You can find them at farmers' markets in late autumn. This is a pudding in the British sense—more like a bread pudding than a silky mousse confection. Serve the pudding with dollops of whipped cream.

MAKES ONE 12-INCH PUDDING

2 pounds persimmons, stems removed

2 cups whole milk

2½ cups all-purpose flour

2 cups dark brown sugar

2 large eggs, well beaten

2 tablespoons unsalted butter, melted

3 teaspoons baking powder

1 teaspoon baking soda

Pinch of salt

Whipped cream, for serving

1. Preheat the oven to 350°F. Spray a 12-inch cast-iron skillet with cooking spray.
2. Combine the persimmons and milk in a large mixing bowl. Using your hands, squeeze the persimmons to free the seeds and skins, allowing the flesh to become mixed with the milk. Pass the mixture through a colander to remove the seeds and skins.
3. Add the remaining ingredients, except the whipped cream, to the milk mixture, stirring until a smooth batter forms. Pour the batter into the prepared skillet and bake for 35 to 40 minutes, or until set. Remove from the oven.
4. Set the pudding aside to cool in the skillet before serving warm or at room temperature.
5. Scoop portions of the pudding from the skillet and serve with dollops of the whipped cream.

Orange Drops

I found this super-simple idea for candy in my great-grandmother's copy of *The White House Cookbook*, which was published in the late nineteenth century. You can make this with any juice—just make sure it is freshly squeezed.

MAKES 3 DOZEN DROPS

1 pound confectioners' sugar, plus more as needed

Freshly squeezed juice of 1 blood orange

1. Dust a sheet of wax paper with confectioners' sugar.
2. Put the juice in a large mixing bowl. Begin stirring in the sugar, a little at a time, until you have a dough that can be shaped by hand (you may be surprised at how much sugar is required).
3. Shape the sugar dough into 1-inch balls and place them on the prepared wax paper.
4. Serve or store the candy in an airtight container at room temperature for up to 6 weeks.

Pear Bread

This spicy quickbread is wonderful with the Sweet Whiskey Butter on the following page. The quantities given will make one loaf in a 7¾-by-3¾-by-2-inch foil loaf pan, which is smaller than a standard loaf pan. If you wish, you can substitute apple for some or all of the pear. You could also add ½ cup of chopped nuts to increase the protein content. Bartlett pears are ripe when they change from green to yellow, and when the neck yields to gentle pressure. An average-size Bartlett yields about 1 cup of diced flesh. If you use smaller pear varieties, you may need more than one fruit.

MAKES 1 SMALL LOAF

⅔ cup granulated sugar

⅓ cup vegetable oil

1 large egg, well beaten

¼ teaspoon vanilla extract

1 cup all-purpose flour

¼ teaspoon baking soda

¼ teaspoon ground cinnamon

¼ teaspoon salt

1 yellow Bartlett pear, peeled, cored, and finely diced

1. Preheat the oven to 300°F. Oil a 7¾-by-3¾-by-2-inch loaf pan.
2. Combine the sugar, oil, egg, and vanilla extract in a large mixing bowl.
3. Whisk together the flour, baking soda, cinnamon, and salt in a separate mixing bowl. Using a large spoon, gradually stir the dry ingredients into the liquid mixture, mixing constantly until a uniform batter forms. Fold in the diced pear.
4. Transfer the batter to the prepared pan. Smooth down the top with the spoon and place in the oven on the middle shelf. Bake for 1½ hours, or until a toothpick inserted into the bread comes out clean. Remove from the oven and set aside to cool in the pan for 10 minutes.
5. Turn out onto a wire rack to cool completely.
6. Serve immediately, or return the cooled bread to the pan and store, covered, at room temperature for up to 3 days.

Sweet Whiskey Butter

Whiskey has a long history in the mountains—most famously, when it was widely produced in illegal stills. New laws have recently allowed small distilleries to return to the region, and they are beginning to release their products. Whiskey turns up in all sorts of recipes around here, and this butter is but one example.

MAKES 1 STICK

8 tablespoons (1 stick) unsalted butter, softened

1½ tablespoons Tennessee whiskey

1 tablespoon sorghum molasses

¼ teaspoon vanilla extract

1. Thoroughly mash the butter with a fork in a mixing bowl. Stir in all of the remaining ingredients until thoroughly blended.

2. Using plastic wrap as an aid, shape the butter into a log. Store up to 1 week in the refrigerator, or wrap the log in foil and store in the freezer for up to 6 months. Thaw overnight in the refrigerator or for about 3 hours at room temperature before using.

Black Walnut Fruit Cake

I developed this recipe for one reason: my cousin's wife would not share her recipe with me! The flavor of black walnuts is unique, and makes this fruit cake different from any other you may have tried. Feel free to substitute other dried fruits, but make sure you include the black walnuts.

MAKES ONE 8½-BY-4½-INCH CAKE

1¾ cups all-purpose flour

½ teaspoon baking powder

½ teaspoon ground cinnamon

¼ teaspoon ground allspice

¼ teaspoon kosher salt

½ cup chopped black walnuts

½ cup raisins

½ cup chopped candied orange peel

½ cup chopped dried apricots

8 tablespoons (1 stick) unsalted butter, softened, plus more for greasing

1 cup dark brown sugar

3 large eggs, room temperature

½ teaspoon vanilla extract

4 ounces gold or dark rum

1. Whisk together the flour, baking powder, cinnamon, allspice, and salt in a medium mixing bowl until thoroughly combined. Set aside.

2. Place the walnuts, raisins, orange peel, and apricots in a second bowl. Add ¼ cup of the flour mixture and toss until evenly coated. Set aside.

3. Preheat the oven to 325°F. Line an 8½-by-4½-inch loaf pan with heavy-duty aluminum foil. Butter the foil well and set the pan aside.

4. Combine the butter and brown sugar in the bowl of a stand mixer fitted with the paddle attachment and mix on low speed until the ingredients are combined. Increase the speed to medium and beat until the mixture is light and fluffy.

5. Combine the eggs and vanilla extract in a small bowl and beat well with a fork.

6. Gradually add the egg mixture to the butter mixture, a third at a time, while the mixer continues to run on medium speed, until a uniform batter forms. Gradually add the flour mixture, a third at a time. Reduce the mixer speed as the batter thickens.

7. When all of the flour mixture has been incorporated, turn off the mixer and remove the bowl. Scrape down the paddle with a rubber spatula and use the spatula to fold the nut and fruit mixture into the batter. Turn the batter several times with the spatula to evenly incorporate the nuts and fruits—the batter will be stiff and sticky.

8. Turn out the batter into the prepared pan. Bake for 1 hour and 35 minutes, or until a tester inserted into the center of the cake comes out with a few wet crumbs attached (the cake will continue to cook after you remove it from the oven). Remove from the oven and allow to cool in the pan for 20 minutes.

9. Turn out the cake onto a rack and allow it to cool completely. Tightly wrap the cooled cake in plastic wrap and set aside at room temperature overnight.

10. Unwrap and puncture the cake through the top in several places with a skewer. Slowly pour the rum over the cake. Tightly rewrap the cake in plastic wrap and then wrap it in aluminum foil. Store in a cool, dark place for 1 week before slicing and serving.

Chapter Six

TOO GOOD TO LEAVE OUT

A few dishes that don't easily fit into the categories in this book have made their way to this chapter—take Pimento Cheese (page 170), for example. The recipe is a close cousin to chilled, mayonnaise-bound salads like egg salad, but it is more often used as a spread or a dip, and it's not really a condiment, either. Biscuits (pages 172 and 173) are an essential accompaniment to many dishes, but absent a chapter devoted to baking, they ended up here. Don't be surprised if some of the recipes in this chapter become favorites. They already are for us.

Pimento Cheese

Spread it on crackers, use it on a sandwich or a burger, or stuff celery with it—pimento cheese may just be the all-purpose spread you have been looking for. And while it *is* mostly all about the cheese, pay attention to the quality of the pimentos and mayonnaise you use. I prefer Dromedary pimentos, from East Tennessee's Moody Dunbar Company, and Duke's Mayonnaise, which hails from Greenville, South Carolina (Greenville lies in the eastern foothills, so we'll count it as part of our Appalachian region). I tested the recipe using smoked Gouda from Sweetwater Valley Creamery in Philadelphia, Tennessee; you can also use a mixture of cheeses, if you wish. Any variety that grates easily will work. This might be a good way to use up a leftover cheese board.

MAKES APPROXIMATELY 2½ CUPS

10 ounces smoked Gouda, freshly grated

2 ounces canned chopped pimentos, undrained

¼ teaspoon freshly ground black pepper

¼ teaspoon Highland Heat Seasoning (page 17)

⅛ teaspoon celery seeds

½ cup mayonnaise, plus more as needed

Combine the cheese, pimentos, black pepper, Highland Heat Seasoning, and celery seeds in a mixing bowl. Gradually add the mayonnaise, stirring it in gently until the mixture reaches a spreadable consistency. Refrigerate until you are ready to serve.

Pimento Cheese Chowder

Pimento Cheese (see facing page) is popular all over the South, and especially so in the mountains. The flavor of this ubiquitous spread is captured in this hearty, warming soup.

MAKES 4 FIRST-COURSE SERVINGS

1 tablespoon unsalted butter

2 large shallots, minced

1 garlic clove, minced

2 tablespoons all-purpose flour

1 cup whole milk

1 cup chicken broth, plus more as needed

½ cup water, plus more as needed

1 pound potatoes, peeled and cut into ½-inch cubes

¼ teaspoon dried thyme

One 3.5- to 4-ounce jar diced pimentos

1 cup freshly grated sharp Cheddar, plus more for garnish

Salt

Freshly ground black pepper

Crumbled cooked bacon, for garnish

Finely sliced scallions, for garnish

1. Melt the butter in a large pot over medium heat. Add the shallots and garlic and cook for 3 minutes, or until the shallots are softened. Stir the flour into the shallot mixture and cook for 30 seconds.

2. While constantly stirring, pour the milk into the shallot mixture in a consistent stream. The soup will thicken quickly; keep stirring.

3. Add the chicken broth, water, potatoes, and thyme and bring to a simmer. Cook, stirring occasionally, for 12 to 15 minutes, or until the potatoes are just cooked. (If the soup gets too thick, add more chicken broth or water.) Add the pimentos and their liquid to the soup and cook for 2 minutes. Remove from the heat.

4. Stir in as much of the grated cheese as you like. Taste for seasoning and add the salt and black pepper as needed. Ladle the soup into warmed bowls. Garnish with the bacon, scallions, and more of the Cheddar and serve.

Easy Buttermilk Biscuits

This simple recipe for biscuits requires real churned buttermilk. If you have local buttermilk available, use it; otherwise, look for top-quality organic buttermilk at the supermarket. The exact amount of buttermilk required varies depending on numerous factors. Use just enough to bring the flour together to form a firm, not sticky, dough. Making good biscuits requires both a light touch and lots of practice. Use your dominant hand to mix the dough, and you'll learn how it feels when it's right.

MAKES 6 BISCUITS

1 cup self-rising flour (see Note)

½ cup (approximately) churned buttermilk

Note: You can make your own self-rising flour, if you prefer. To each 1 cup of all-purpose flour, add 1¼ teaspoons of double-acting baking powder and ¼ teaspoon of kosher salt. Mix thoroughly with a wire whisk or sift the ingredients together before storing in an airtight container at room temperature. Baking powder is best used within 6 months of opening, so make your self-rising flour with fresh baking powder and use the flour within 6 months for best results.

1. Preheat the oven to 400°F.
2. Place the flour in a large mixing bowl. Using your dominant hand to mix, fold the buttermilk into the flour, a little bit at a time, just until the dough forms a pliable mass. If it becomes sticky, add a little more flour.
3. Turn out the dough onto a parchment paper-lined baking sheet and pat it into a rectangle about ½ inch thick. Using a sharp knife or pastry blade, cut the dough once down the middle along its length, and then cut twice across, making 6 biscuits. Do not separate the biscuits.
4. Bake for 10 to 15 minutes, or until golden brown on top. Remove from the oven.
5. Serve immediately.

Cat Head Biscuits

Big as a cat's head: that's how you should make these easy, high-rising biscuits. Perfect for soaking up gravy, they can also enclose an array of sandwich fillings, sweet or savory. This batter is heavier than that of the previous recipe. I added a little extra baking powder to make sure the biscuits turn out nice and fluffy.

MAKES 6 BIG BISCUITS

2 cups self-rising flour (see Note, page 172)

6 tablespoons vegetable oil

1½ teaspoons granulated sugar

½ teaspoon baking powder

1 cup buttermilk or a little less

1 tablespoon unsalted butter, melted

1. Preheat the oven to 450°F.

2. Using a large spoon, stir together the flour, oil, sugar, and baking powder in a large mixing bowl. Add the buttermilk, a little bit at a time, mixing just until the dough holds together without becoming sticky.

3. Turn out the dough onto a floured surface and roll out to about a ¾-inch thickness. Using a 2½-inch round cutter, cut out 5 biscuits. Gently recombine the remaining dough scraps to make 1 more biscuit.

4. Transfer the biscuits to an ungreased baking sheet and brush them with the melted butter. Bake for 10 to 15 minutes, or until golden brown on top (watch carefully to prevent burning). Remove from the oven.

5. Serve immediately.

Deviled Eggs

Hard-cooked eggs have no doubt been a transportable food since they were invented, and no picnic in the mountains would be complete without a platter of deviled eggs. They're a great appetizer for any time, and deviled eggs have long been a standard on our family Thanksgiving table. Here, I have reduced the yield to 6 stuffed eggs, but the recipe can be easily multiplied if you have a crowd. Around here, most people have one or more serving plates made just for deviled eggs, with appropriate egg-shaped depressions. Often, these are treasured family heirlooms. The shape of those depressions, by the way, should lay to rest the controversy over whether to split the eggs lengthwise or crosswise: lengthwise wins. Deviled egg plates are immensely helpful for transporting the eggs without lots of sliding around on the plate. Deviled eggs win more compliments when made with Sweet Lime Cucumber Pickles (page 3).

MAKES 6 EGG HALVES

3 large eggs, hard boiled and peeled (see page 176)

1 teaspoon minced sweet pickles

½ teaspoon sweet pickle juice

⅛ teaspoon Homemade Beer Mustard (page 16)

Pinch of salt

Freshly ground black pepper

1 teaspoon to 1 tablespoon mayonnaise

Ground paprika

1. Slice the eggs in half lengthwise. Remove the yolks to a mixing bowl and reserve the whites on a serving plate.

2. Add the pickles, pickle juice, and Homemade Beer Mustard to the yolks and season with the salt and black pepper to taste. Mash the yolks with a fork and stir until all of the ingredients are well combined and the mixture is uniform. Add the mayonnaise, 1 teaspoon at a time, to thin the mixture to the consistency you prefer.

3. Spoon the mixture into the egg-white halves or put the mixture into a plastic bag, snip off one corner, and pipe the mixture into the whites. Sprinkle the stuffed eggs with the paprika.

4. Serve immediately or store until ready to use; the eggs can be made 1 day before using and should be stored in an airtight container in the refrigerator.

Note: Deviled eggs can be fancied up with all sorts of garnishes and toppings—bits of bacon, slices of olive, capers, or a piece of smoked salmon can all add variety to the plate. Use your imagination!

HARD-BOILED EGGS

Older eggs are easier to peel than fresh eggs, so remember that when choosing which eggs to boil up. Choose a pan that will comfortably fit (in a single layer) all the eggs you intend to cook. Place the eggs in the pan and cover them with water by 1 inch. Place the pan over medium-high heat and add ½ teaspoon of baking soda, which helps the egg membrane adhere to the shell instead of the egg white.

When the water reaches a full boil, cover the pan and remove it from the heat. Set aside for 20 minutes.

Using a slotted spoon, transfer the eggs to an ice bath and set aside for 5 minutes.

Crack the eggs on a hard surface and then roll each one around under your palm to break the shell in multiple places. Peel each egg, beginning at the large end. Peeled hard-boiled eggs will keep in a covered container in the refrigerator for up to 2 weeks.

Tomato Gravy

Delicious on pork or chicken, or simply ladled over biscuits or corn bread, tomato gravy recalls the flavor of summertime tomatoes, all captured in a jar. Try it with my Stone-Ground Corn Bread with Corn Kernels (page 39) or Meatloaf with Wild Mushrooms (page 102). If you do not have home-canned tomatoes, choose any good-quality commercially canned tomatoes for this recipe. Don't be heavy handed with the seasonings, or else the result will be more like spaghetti sauce.

MAKES APPROXIMATELY 1 CUP

1 tablespoon unsalted butter

½ cup finely diced yellow onion

¼ teaspoon salt

¼ teaspoon freshly ground black pepper

½ teaspoon minced fresh thyme

2 teaspoons all-purpose flour

½ cup drained, chopped canned tomatoes, juice reserved

½ cup whole (not 2%) milk

1. Melt the butter over medium-low heat in a medium saucepan. Add the onion and cook, stirring often, for 2 minutes. Stir in the salt, black pepper, and thyme and cook for 5 minutes. Stir in the flour and cook for 2 minutes. Add the tomatoes and cook for 5 minutes.

2. Reduce the heat to low, stir in the milk, and simmer gently for 2 minutes. Remove from the heat. Taste for seasoning and adjust as needed.

3. Serve immediately or store in a covered container in the refrigerator.

ANDREW JOHNSON

Andrew Johnson, the seventeenth president of the United States, fled an abusive apprenticeship in his hometown of Raleigh, North Carolina, and eventually settled in Greeneville, Tennessee in 1826. Despite being from one of the Confederate states, Johnson remained loyal to the Union—as were many of his neighbors in East Tennessee.

As president, Johnson was vilified by the Radical Republicans in part because he refused to treat his fellow East Tennesseans as harshly as Congress had wanted, and in part because of his attitude toward the recently emancipated former slaves. The discord culminated in his impeachment, but he was acquitted by a single vote. Admired as he was by many in East Tennessee, Johnson was subsequently elected to the United States Senate in 1875 but died shortly thereafter.

Often derided as the "worst" president, owing to his views on slavery and African Americans, Johnson has nevertheless been admired for his steadfast vision of constitutional government. Volumes have been devoted to debating Johnson's position in history, and the Civil War and its aftermath were among the most difficult times in the nation's history. Johnson's legacy will remain controversial.

What's not in doubt, however, is Johnson's preference for buckwheat pancakes for breakfast. Thanks to his daughter Martha, who died in 1901, the actual recipe he enjoyed has been handed down. It required a sourdough starter and considerable effort—no doubt appropriate for breakfast at the White House.

Buckwheat Pancakes

Buckwheat used to be more popular than it is these days, but now that people are beginning to rediscover unusual grains, buckwheat is making a comeback. Serve these pancakes with butter and sorghum or maple syrup along with a side of Benton's Smoky Mountain Bacon. You can order Benton's online (see Sources, page 183).

MAKES 12 PANCAKES

1½ cups buttermilk

1 cup all-purpose flour

½ cup buckwheat flour

2 large eggs

3 tablespoons unsalted butter, melted

3 tablespoons granulated sugar

1½ teaspoons baking powder

½ teaspoon baking soda

½ teaspoon salt

1. Preheat the oven to 200°F.

2. Combine all of the ingredients in the jar of a blender and process for 10 seconds, or until combined. Refrigerate the blender jar for 1 hour to overnight to allow the batter to rest. If you do not have a blender, vigorously beat together all of the ingredients with a wire whisk in a medium mixing bowl and then refrigerate the batter for 1 hour to overnight.

3. Lightly grease a griddle or a large cast-iron skillet over medium heat. Ladle the batter, ⅓ cup at a time, onto the griddle, taking care not to crowd the pancakes (they will spread to about a 6-inch diameter).

4. When bubbles appear on the tops of each pancake and the edges look dry, turn each pancake with a spatula and cook for about 2 minutes, until the other side is browned. As each pancake is cooked, transfer it to a plate and keep the plate in the warm oven. Repeat until all the pancakes have been cooked, and remove from the heat.

5. Serve immediately.

All-American Munch Mix

Most of the ingredients in this tasty, crunchy snack mix would have been familiar to Native Americans centuries ago.

MAKES APPROXIMATELY 4 CUPS

4 ounces raw American hazelnuts

2 ounces wild or Georgia pecans

2 ounces raw pepitas (pumpkin seeds)

2 ounces raw sunflower kernels

1 tablespoon sunflower oil

1 tablespoon sourwood honey (see Note)

1 teaspoon coarse sea salt

¼ teaspoon ancho chili powder

¼ teaspoon garlic powder

¼ teaspoon onion powder

¼ teaspoon sweet paprika

1½ ounces dried cranberries

1. Preheat the oven to 375°F.

2. Place the raw hazelnuts in a heavy, cast-iron skillet and roast them in the oven for 10 minutes. Remove from the oven and reduce the oven temperature to 300°F.

3. Transfer the hazelnuts to a kitchen towel and set aside to cool slightly.

4. Rub the hazelnuts vigorously between your hands to remove the skins. Discard the skins and reserve the hazelnuts.

5. Combine the pepitas and sunflower kernels in a large mixing bowl and set aside.

6. Combine the oil, honey, salt, chili powder, garlic powder, onion powder, and paprika in a small microwavable bowl. Microwave for about 30 seconds, or until warm and fully combined. (Alternatively, stir the ingredients together in a small saucepan over low heat until the salt dissolves.) Drizzle the hot liquid over the seed mixture, tossing it until well coated.

7. Scatter the coated seeds in a thin, single layer on a parchment paper-lined baking sheet. Bake for 15 minutes, and then remove from the oven to stir.

8. Return to the oven for 15 minutes, and then remove from the oven to stir.

9. Add the toasted hazelnuts to the baking sheet, stir, and return to the oven for

15 minutes, or until the pepitas begin to brown. Remove from the oven and set aside to cool slightly.

10. Add the cranberries to the baking sheet and stir until combined. Set aside to cool to room temperature.

11. Serve immediately or store in an airtight container kept at room temperature for up to 2 months.

Note: Sourwood honey, made by bees from the nectar of sourwood tree blossoms, is light in color with a distinctive flavor. Widely available in the mountain South, it can also be ordered online (see Sources).

SOURCES

FOOD PRODUCTS

Listed here are some of the companies that make the food of the southern Appalachians accessible to the rest of the world. They provide authentic ingredients and plenty of additional recipes—both new and traditional. New producers arrive on the scene on a regular basis, and no list like this can ever be considered complete. You can find additional regional products via an Internet search.

ANSON MILLS
1922 Gervais Street
Columbia, SC 29201
(803) 467-4122
ansonmills.com
Purveyors of Southern heirloom grains, legumes, and other products.

BENTON'S SMOKY MOUNTAIN COUNTRY HAMS
2603 US-411
Madisonville, TN 37354
bentonscountryham.com
Allan Benton makes country ham the old-fashioned way, from heritage hogs. His bacon was called the "finest in the world" by New York celebrity chef David Chang.

BLACKBERRY FARM
1471 West Millers Cove Road
Walland, TN 37886
(865) 984-8166
blackberryfarmshop.com
Blackberry Farm is an ultra-luxe mountain resort often credited with igniting the Appalachian cuisine craze. Many of the farm's handmade products are available on its website.

LAKESIDE MILLS, INC.
PO Box #230
Rutherfordton, NC 28139
(828) 286-4866
lakesidemills.com
Millers of flour, cornmeal, and grits, Lakeside Mills maintains the old tradition of stone-grinding corn to preserve its special taste.

MOODY DUNBAR, INC.
PO Box 6048
Johnson City, TN 37602-6048
moodydunbar.com
When Moody Dunbar started selling vegetable seeds to supplement his income, he never dreamed his project would become a multimillion-dollar company producing pimentos, roasted peppers, and sweet potatoes for a worldwide market.

SUNBURST TROUT FARMS

314 Industrial Park Drive

Waynesville, NC 28786

(800) 673-3051

sunbursttrout.com

Pristine water and an all-natural diet have helped this company produce top-quality rainbow trout since 1948.

STRANGE HONEY FARM

245 South Hwy 107

Del Rio, TN 37727

(423) 613-0438

Representing numerous beekeepers and offering a wide selection of honey and honey products, this regionally distributed company has recently added mountain-grown sorghum syrup to its offerings.

SWAGGERTY'S FARM

2827 Swaggerty Road

Kodak, TN 37764

swaggertys.com

For real mountain taste in country pork sausage, Swaggerty's is the source.

WHITE LILY FLOUR

whitelily.com

Once exclusively made in Knoxville, Tennessee, White Lily is now owned and produced by Smuckers, the company famous for its jams and jellies. This exceptionally fine, high-starch flour is essential for biscuits, pie crust, and other Southern-style baked goods. If you can't find it locally, you can order from the company's website.

HEIRLOOM VEGETABLE SEEDS

The people of the mountain South have been avid seed savers for generations. Today, dozens of heirloom varieties remain available to intrepid gardeners. Following are some companies that specialize in heirloom Appalachian vegetable seeds.

BAKER CREEK HEIRLOOM SEEDS

rareseeds.com

SOUTHERN EXPOSURE SEED EXCHANGE

southernexposure.com

SOW TRUE SEED

sowtrueseed.com

CRAFT BEER

You can learn about the numerous craft breweries in East Tennessee and western North Carolina by visiting their respective brewers guild websites.

TENNESSEE CRAFT BREWERS GUILD

tncraftbrewers.org

NORTH CAROLINA CRAFT BREWERS GUILD

ncbeer.org

FURTHER READING

More information about the colorful and fascinating early history of the southern mountains can be obtained from these books.

Arthur, John Preston. *Western North Carolina: A History from 1730-1913.* Johnson City, TN: Overmountain Press, 1996.

Clayton, LaReine Warden, and Jane Gray Buchanan. *Stories of Early Inns and Taverns of the East Tennessee Country.* Nashville: National Society of the Colonial Dames of America in the State of Tennessee, 1995.

Deaderick, Lucile. *Heart of the Valley: A History of Knoxville, Tennessee.* Knoxville, TN: The East Tennessee Historical Society, 1976.

Dykeman, Wilma. *The French Broad.* Newport, TN: Wakestone Books, 1999.

———. *The Tall Woman.* New York: Holt, Rinehart and Winston, 1971.

Rothrock, Mary Utopia. *The French-Broad Holston Country, A History of Knox County, Tennessee.* Knoxville, TN: East Tennessee Historical Society, 1946.

Apple Stack Cake (page 148)

INDEX